GREEK ISLAND MYTHOLOGY

By the same author and published by NEL

LAND OF ZEUS: MYTHS OF THE GREEK GODS AND HEROES

Greek Island Mythology

Stephanie Dowrick

NEW ENGLISH LIBRARY
TIMES MIRROR

To the memory of C. S. Lewis who once remarked that the power of the myths was such that it could be felt even through the most atrocious of modern summaries.

First published in Great Britain by New English Library Ltd., 1974
© Stephanie Dowrick 1974

*

FIRST NEL PAPERBACK EDITION MARCH 1974

*

*NEL Books are published by
New English Library Limited from Barnard's Inn, Holborn, London, E.C.1.
Made and printed in Great Britain by Hunt Barnard Printing Ltd., Aylesbury, Bucks.*

45001886 5

CONTENTS

Introduction

GREEK ISLAND MYTHOLOGY has been written to give the reader, and especially the visitor to Greece, a glimpse of the endless richness of one of the oldest cultures in the world and of the life that was lived on and around the Greek islands in the past.

Some of this life was real; some imagined. Many myths have a basis in reality, but others sprang wholly from the minds of an imaginative and immensely creative people who were looking for satisfactory explanations for the creation and meaning of their world.

The myths that were born in the minds of these early Greeks have survived through centuries of development of European culture, even to the present day, making them as personally relevant to everyone who has been touched by Western culture as they are to the Greeks who now live in this beautiful and historic country.

The myths have travelled through centuries of telling and re-telling. They are not history, and not therefore bound by the constraints of accuracy. In each telling their shape inevitably moves somewhat and different versions now exist. There is no right nor wrong version, though some are more generally accepted and in nearly every case I have presented this, just as when there is dispute as to the geographical setting of a myth I have placed it on the island most usually associated with it.

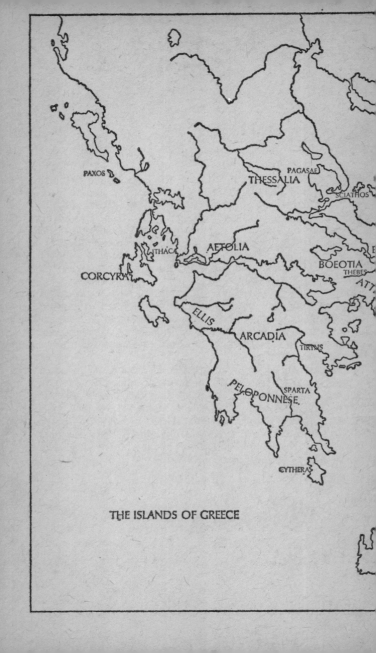

THE ISLANDS OF GREECE

IN THE BEGINNING . . .

First there was Chaos

> . . . the vast immeasurable abyss,
> Outrageous as a sea, dark, wasteful, wild,
> Up from the bottom turned by furious winds
> And surging waves, as mountains, to assault
> Heav'n's highth, and with the centre mix the pole.
>
> Milton

In the beginning of time there was nothing but a dark mass called Chaos. Hidden in Chaos were all the elements which now exist separately: the earth, the sky, darkness and light, water and fire. But then they did not have a separate form.

Finally Chaos split apart. Nature created order, dividing earth from heaven and placing in heaven the sun, the moon and the five planets, while on earth water separated from the ground, and divisions were made between hot, cold and temperate zones. Mountains and rivers were formed and covered in trees and grass.

On land beasts walked and in the waters fishes swam.

Last of all Nature made man.

*　　*　　*

Or perhaps man was made by Prometheus, a Titan whose name means forethought, for it is said that with Athene's support Prometheus made men out of clay and then Athene breathed life into him.

For a long time there were only men on earth then Zeus became angry with these men, and more especially with the Titan, who was the first to give fire to men, something which had previously belonged only to gods. And so Zeus decided to take revenge.

Zeus's revenge was, quite simply, to order Hephaestus to make a woman out of clay. She was then brought to life by the breath of the four winds, and dressed and made beautiful by the goddesses. Her name was Pandora.

Pandora was sent as a gift to Epimetheus, who was Prometheus's brother. His name means afterthought.

Epimetheus had been warned by Prometheus that under no circumstances was he to accept a gift from Zeus, so although he was charmed at the sight of the lovely Pandora he told Hermes, who was accompanying the girl, that he had to refuse.

Zeus was furious that Epimetheus could dare to decline his gift, but knew at once that the wisdom behind the refusal was not Epimetheus's, but Prometheus's. So he devised for Prometheus a most horrible punishment. He had the Titan chained to a pillar high in the mountains, naked and exposed.

As Prometheus hung helpless and defenceless a vicious vulture would gnaw and tear at his liver all day long. Then next day it would begin again, for during the night, Prometheus's liver would once more have grown whole.

Epimetheus was so alarmed at his brother's fate that he told Zeus he had changed his mind and would accept Pandora as a gift.

At first all went well, for she was a sweet and lovely girl, but she was also extremely curious and the object that most enflamed her curiosity was a box which contained all the Spites: Sickness, Anger, Madness, Vice, Passion, Senility. Each had been placed there by a god and though Epimetheus knew that on no account should Pandora open the box he was unable to restrain her, and one day when his back was turned she could resist no longer, opened the lid, and all those evils which plague men still today, came flying out.

The realisation of these torments was so frightful that it is certain men would have committed suicide then and there except that also imprisoned in the box was Delusive Hope, which continued and continues to sustain men, even in the face of the realities of evil.

*   *   *

But before Zeus or Prometheus or Pandora and her curiosity, there was only a god of the sky called Uranus, or perhaps he was the sky, or heaven. The goddess of the earth was called Gaea, warm full-breasted Mother Earth; perhaps she was the earth?

Uranus and Gaea had eighteen children; six ugly and twelve

beautiful. These early gods all looked rather like men and women, although rather more beautiful than most, and on a much larger scale. So when Uranus and Gaea had six children who were monstrously ugly they were extremely distressed, though Mother Earth loved them despite their deformities. Three were Cyclopes, each with only one great eye, larger than a cart-wheel, sitting in the middle of a vast forehead. The other three had two eyes apiece, but each had a hundred hands. These were called the Hundred-handed Giants.

His six ugly offspring were so abhorrent to Uranus that he banished them from his sight, sending them to Tartarus, the deep dark underworld which is as far down through earth as the earth is from the sky – a distance it would take a stone nine days to fall. Mother Earth missed her ugly first born and didn't forget them despite the fact that she and Uranus then had their twelve beautiful children, six Titans and six Titanesses. Among these were Cronus, who was to be their leader*; Rhea, his sister and wife; Atlas, who was to be condemned to hold the weight of the world on his shoulders; Oceanus, the stream which encircles the world; Thetis, his wife; Hyperion, father of the sun, moon and dawn; Mnemosyne, whose name means memory and Prometheus, creator of the first men, although some did insist that the first men sprang from serpents' teeth.

Gaea's resentment towards Uranus for his behaviour to the Cyclopes and the Hundred-handed Giants smouldered and grew to such an extent that she encouraged Cronus, her son, in his ambitions and conspired with him to take over the leadership from Uranus, on condition that he freed the six from Tartarus.

Cronus readily agreed to Mother Earth's condition and then one day as Uranus lay on his couch Cronus and his brothers crept up behind their father and while the others held him down Cronus castrated Uranus with a sickle, holding the genitals high in his left hand so the blood which fell fertilized Mother Earth once more and she gave birth to the Three Furies, avengers of patricide who were quite frightful to look at with writhing snakes for hair and eyes that wept blood, and the three Giants, yet another race of monsters. The genitals themselves fell into the sea, foam gathered around them and from this foam, Aphrodite sprang; a somewhat strange beginning for the goddess of Love.

With Cronus in power the Titans quickly released the Cyclopes and Hundred-handed Giants but were so alarmed by their ap-

* His Roman name is Saturn.

pearance and strength that they just as quickly returned them to Tartarus.

Cronus now married his sister Rhea, but as it had been prophesied by Uranus when Cronus had maimed him so hideously, that Cronus in his turn would be dethroned by a son, Cronus swallowed every child that Rhea bore him.

Five children born to Cronus and Rhea were swallowed in this way, but when the sixth was due to be born Rhea was determined to outwit Cronus so she had the baby in secret, took it to Crete, and gave Cronus a stone wrapped in swaddling clothes to swallow instead, and he accepted the deception without question.

After a year or so the child hidden on Crete was quite grown up and came back to his mother Rhea, ready to take revenge on Cronus on behalf of his swallowed brothers and sisters.

This child was Zeus – the greatest of all the gods.

Together Rhea and Zeus made a plan. As Cronus would not recognise Zeus he would be introduced to Cronus as a cup-bearer and would give to his father an emetic drink, but mixed with honey so that Cronus would not suspect what he was drinking.

All went as planned and when Cronus had drained the cup to the bottom he was violently ill, and out from his stomach came first the stone he had swallowed thinking that it was Zeus, then the five other children: Hestia, Demeter, Hera, Hades and Poseidon. These children were quite unharmed by their pause in Cronus's stomach, and emerged militant and well. The sisters and brothers were extremely grateful to Zeus and unanimously chose him as their leader in the war which they now declared against the Titans.

Perhaps Cronus was so overcome by the bewildering chain of events that he could no longer cope, or perhaps he really was just past his prime, but as their leader the Titans elected not Cronus but Atlas. And so the war began.

For ten long years this fierce war waged, back and forth between Zeus and his brothers and sisters – the Olympians from their home on Mount Olympus – and Atlas and his brothers and sisters – the Titans from their base on Mount Orthrys. The Olympians were outnumbered but Mother Earth was on their side and wisely suggested to her grandson Zeus that he should enlist the support of her ugly children who would willingly give their help against the beautiful Titans who had so callously betrayed them when Cronus was fighting to depose Uranus.

Zeus followed Mother Earth's advice and he and his brothers went down to Tartarus to free the Hundred-handed Giants, and the Cyclopes.

The arrival of this great trio was greeted with huge delight and the Cyclopes presented each Olympian brother with a gift which was to play a vitally significant and important part not only in the ensuing battle, but also in the mighty years which were to follow victory.

To Zeus went the magnificent and fearful thunderbolt; to Hades a helmet of darkness which would allow him to move unseen, and to Poseidon went the trident, a three-pronged spear.

Back to Olympus the brothers went, carrying their gifts and accompanied by the Hundred-handed Giants and the Cyclopes. Then, after a brief counsel of war, the three Olympians struck.

Wearing his helmet of invisibility Hades stole into the room where Cronus rested and stole all the weapons which lay beside him. Poseidon then leapt into the room and moved as if he would strike Cronus with his trident and while Cronus was distracted (and trembling with fear) Zeus entered from another corner and struck Cronus down with his thunderbolt.

The Hundred-handed Giants had their great moment of triumph and revenge for using every single one of their hands they pelted the Titans with stones, banishing all except Atlas to a British island in the west, (the farthest end of the known world). For Atlas as the war leader a very special punishment was reserved. The weight of the world was placed on his shoulders and as he could neither stretch up nor move he would never again find comfort.

The Titanesses were spared, for generally they had shown their sympathies to be with the Olympians.

It was now time for the victorious gods to divide the universe between them so from a helmet they drew lots. Hades won the underworld, dark and gloomy Tartarus; Poseidon won the sea and all underwater rivers. But the greatest prize of all, lordship over the sky, went to Zeus, now marked as the leader of all the gods.

When the war was over Mother Earth quickly realised that she had gained precisely nothing for while her ugly children were now free, the Titans were not, guarded as they were by the Hundred-handed Ones on the British Island. So yet another war began, again incited by Mother Earth and this time between the Olympians and the Giants, hideous monsters of great strength and courage which she had borne from the drops of blood which fell from Uranus's severed genitals when Cronus held them high over her body.

These Giants tore great rocks out of the earth and threw them up into the sky, but from the height and safety of Mount Olympus the Olympians looked down and laughed at them

So the Giants decided a new strategy was necessary and an attempt should be made to reach Mount Olympus, or at least, to get within reasonable aiming distance.

With all their combined and considerable strength the giants then uprooted one mountain and rolled it on top of another to form a huge ladder as high as Olympus itself.

But they had reckoned without Zeus's great thunderbolt which he directed against the bottom mountain tumbling it down again and bringing the upper mountain with it. The gods were now angry enough to engage the Giants in an extremely serious battle which lasted for a long day before the gods at last won a complete victory, crushing each of the Giants beneath a mountain. One giant tried to escape by sea but Athene, Zeus's daughter, tore off a three-cornered piece of land and threw it after him, hitting him on the back and burying him beneath it. This became the island of Sicily.

The giants were not dead, but thoroughly buried, though from time to time they attempted to turn, and rumbled and shook the earth above them.

Mother Earth was still not at peace and she next lay with Tartarus, the underworld, and conceived the most horrible creature of all, the Typhon, which crawled out of a great crack in her body.

The Typhon can scarcely be imagined for it had a hundred serpent heads each with eyes that shot out fire and a mouth that expelled flaming rocks; from each head came an extraordinary, and different, voice, sometimes like a bellowing bull, sometimes a whistling which would echo in the mountains, sometimes the painful whimpering of a young puppy. The Typhon's arms when outstretched were each ten miles long and ended not in hands but more serpents' heads. His wings were so great that they could block out the sun, and below the thighs he twisted and coiled like the most loathsome of serpents.

Some accounts tell us that the Typhon terrified the Olympians so greatly that they all fled to Egypt, disguised as animals. Zeus became a ram; Apollo, a raven; Ares, a boar; Hermes, an ibis (a wading bird with a curved bill which was once worshipped by the ancient Egyptians); Dionysus, a goat; Artemis, a cat; Hera, a cow; Aphrodite, a fish.

But Zeus was not really a coward and Athene, who had refused to hide under the guise of an animal, taunted and provoked him to such an extent that he soon returned to Olympus and began to rain thunderbolts against the Typhon.

The whole earth shook fearfully with the thunder and lightning that flashed from end to end and when Zeus attacked the Typhon, slashing at it with a great sickle, it was put to flight; though not for long.

On the borders of Syria the Typhon suddenly turned on the pursuing Zeus and despite its injuries fought with the god a most terrible battle.

Zeus was as brave as he had ever been, but the Typhon wound his hideous coils around the god, and having overcome him, took the sickle which was Zeus's only weapon. He then pinned Zeus to the ground and cut out the sinews of his hands and feet before thrusting him into a cave. Zeus was both crippled and defeated.

Typhon then left the god, though not before burying the stolen sinews in the depths of a bear skin, guarded by Typhon's sister-monster called Delphyna who was half serpent and half woman.

The Olympians were shocked and amazed at the news of Zeus's unprecedented defeat, and at once made their plan to help him, sending Hermes and Pan to the cave where he lay.

Pan startled Delphyna with the most extraordinary shout she had ever heard and while she was distracted Hermes, the cleverest of thieves, plunged his hand into the bear's skin and found the sinews. The gods then released Zeus and replaced the sinews where they belonged.

Now Zeus was determined to teach the Typhon a final lesson. In his chariot drawn by winged horses he went to Mount Nysa where the Typhon waited.

There the Typhon was offered the food of mortals by the Three Fates who told the creature that they wanted to help him to regain his strength, though in fact they knew that this food would only weaken him. Nevertheless, despite the Fates' ruse, the Typhon fought valiantly and well against Zeus for a second time, resisting the thunderbolts and fleeing to Thrace where he picked up mountains to hurl at Zeus. But Zeus deflected these with his great thunderbolts and the mountains boomeranged back on the Typhon, wounding him hideously, though he still found strength to run on to Sicily, leaving behind him as he went streams of blood.

In Sicily it was Zeus who looked to the mountains as weapons, and picking up Mount Aetna he hurled it at the Typhon, burying him beneath it, though the mountain shook and belched fire for many years afterwards. (This is the highest volcanic mountain in Europe, now called Mount Etna.)

Mother Earth was then forced to acknowledge the strength of the Olympians, and to find some peace with them.

A GATHERING OF GODS

The six gods born to Cronus and Rhea were these:

Zeus

Zeus, last born, but leader of the gods. His name means 'bright' and he is always associated with the sky, over which he ruled; the weather, and because of its association with the weather, the fertility of the soil. Kings were said to derive their power from him and he was believed to take an active interest in political affairs.

Zeus was associated with the oak tree, the most majestic of all trees and of course with his thunderbolt, given to him by the Cyclopes. The concept of Zeus's thunderbolt was an ancient attempt to explain lightning, and it is interesting to note that in two areas where Zeus was most fervently worshipped, namely Arcadia and Dodona, the many oak trees which grew there were frequently subjected to electrical storms, and split or burned by lightning.

Roman name: Jupiter

Poseidon

Poseidon, second in power only to Zeus, ruled the sea and all underground streams, but never quite overcame his jealousy of Zeus's greater power. He too was associated with fertility, because of the water which he was thought to control, and also with earthquakes which the early Greeks thought were due to the water undermining the ground. Indeed it is with earthquakes rather than the sea that Poseidon may first have been associated, and he was often called 'Earthshaker'.

The concept of his appearance is majestic, but wilder than that of Zeus, and he was generally thought to be even more fickle and difficult to please than his more important brother, taking strong likes and (as in the case of Odysseus) even stronger dislikes.

Poseidon is associated too with horses and he is sometimes credited with having created the first horse – in a contest with Athene when competing for Athens he is said to have plunged his trident into the Acropolis and brought forth a horse, though others say that it was a well. However, neither horse nor well could compete with Athene's entry, the first olive tree, and it was she who won the city.

Roman name: Neptune

Hades

Hades, ruler of the Underworld, Tartarus, (which is sometimes known as Hades) was a far less flamboyant character than either of his brothers. Unlike Poseidon who constantly left his underground home to involve himself with the activities on Mount Olympus, Hades rarely left Tartarus and took his responsibilities to the dead very seriously indeed.

He was never in any way regarded as a 'devil', but rather as a stern, but unerringly just god who neither expected nor gave favours. Temples were never dedicated to him as they were to Zeus or Poseidon.

Tartarus itself was seen as being divided into three parts: the Asphodel Meadows where souls were sent which were neither good nor evil; the punishment fields for those who were judged to be serious wrongdoers, and the Elysian Fields for the extremely virtuous.

The Asphodel Meadows is where the souls of the dead heroes were thought to wander purposelessly in the rather cheerless atmosphere, their one pleasure being to drink the libations of blood poured to them by the living which they would drink to feel temporarily like real men once more.

Nearby these meadows was the palace of Hades where he lived for six months of the year with Queen Persephone (the winter) and six months alone (summer) when she returned to the world of the living.

In this area too was said to be the pool of Lethe where the common ghosts would drink, though those that had been in Tartarus for some time would choose instead to drink from the pool of Memory.

Those ghosts unfortunate enough to be in the punishment fields each had to endure a separate punishment, related to the evil of their lives. Sisyphus, for example, the cunning founder of Corinth, was ordered to roll a huge stone up a steep hill. But after pushing and panting and sweating, and *almost* reaching the top, the stone would run back down the hill, and he would be forced to begin all over again.

Elysium was eternally happy, eternally bright. Music, laughter and games went on endlessly and those souls fortunate enough to find their home there, could at any time choose to be returned to earth. This part of the underworld was ruled by Cronus, Hades's father.

Roman name: Pluto

Hestia

Hestia was goddess of the Hearth, but her role was gradually taken over by the other more vigorous goddesses, though meals usually began and ended with an offering to her. Like Athena and Artemis she was a virgin goddess.

Each city had a public hearth which was sacred to her with a fire which was never allowed to die out and in Rome, under her Roman name of Vesta, the city fire was kept by the Vestal virgins.

Originally one of the twelve Olympians she is said to have gratefully given up her place to Dionysus when Zeus wished to place him at their table, and to have quickly faded into even greater obscurity.

Roman name: Vesta

Demeter

Demeter, the corn-goddess, is not always included among the Twelve, though she was extremely important to the Greeks who acknowledged that her corn sustained life, and the first corn field marked the beginning of settled life on earth. Because sowing and reaping was women's work it was natural that corn should be entrusted to the care of a goddess and not a god. Her chief festival was celebrated at harvest time, and every five years, in September, there would be a great celebration in her honour which would last for nine days. Part of this festival took place in the street where there would be singing, dancing and rejoicing, but another part was held in secret in the great temple at Eleusis near Athens. This worship was called the Eleusian Mysteries and was especially venerated throughout the Greek and Roman world.

Roman name: Ceres

Hera

Hera who married her brother Zeus, is known in mythology chiefly for the role she plays as an excessively watchful and jealous wife, quick and spiteful in her revenge.

Despite the fact that she personified some of the worst of wifely traits (and married Zeus only when tricked and trapped) she was the patroness of married women and the protector of marriage.

Her role both independently and as Zeus's wife was extremely important and she was worshipped by men as well as women.

Roman name: Juno

Among the later-born gods were:

Athena

Athena, Zeus's favourite child, sprang fully grown and fully armed from his head. She was, in a uniquely indirect way, a daughter of Metis the Titaness. Zeus was eager to make love to Metis who was equally keen that he should not. She changed herself into many shapes, trying to evade him but without success, and at last he captured her and made her pregnant. Then it was predicted that although the child she expected was a girl, if Metis was to bear another child, it would be a son, who would be greater than his father.

Zeus was exceedingly alarmed by the prediction and to prevent it coming true swallowed Metis, which some say ended her life, though others believe that she continued to advise him from the depths of his stomach.

After some time Zeus began to be plagued by raging headaches which refused to abate until finally Hermes diagnosed the problem and arranged for Hephaestus to split open Zeus's head, and out came Athene.

She was a most charming goddess, patroness of weaving and inventor of many useful things including the ship, the chariot, the flute and the earthenware pot. Although goddess of war she took no pleasure in fighting except in the most honourable of causes and then she was as fearless as Ares and twice as just. As important as her role as goddess of war was her role as goddess of the city and protector of civilised life.

Athens was her particular city.

Roman name: Minerva

Apollo

Apollo was always associated with beauty and grace, and was god of music. He was also a symbol of light and reason. As god of truth he took over the shrine of the Delphic Oracle, first seizing Pan and forcing the goat-god to teach him the gift of prophecy and then capturing the Delphic Oracle, making the Pythoness (the priestess) his own servant.

Visitors to the Delphic Oracle would put their questions to the priestess who would then go into a trance before replying. This state of trance was deepened by a vapour which rose out of the rock over which she sat, perched on a three-legged stool.

Apollo was the first god to fall in love with a boy, though many other stories recount his pursuit of women, a reflection of the prevalence of practice and acceptance of bi-sexuality in ancient Greek times.

Roman name: Apollo

Artemis

Artemis was Apollo's sister, like him a child of Zeus and Leto, and worshipped with him on the island of Delos.

Artemis was the virgin huntress, associated with wild animals and uncultivated areas. She is said to have asked Zeus, at the age of three, for eternal virginity and a bow and arrow like Apollo's.

This goddess was protectress of the young, and although herself a virgin, patroness of child-birth, probably because she was credited with having helped Leto give birth to Apollo nine days after her own birth.

Roman name: Diana

Aphrodite

Aphrodite, goddess of love and desire, was held in extremely high regard by the sensual Greeks, and was worshipped everywhere that Greek was spoken. Her name comes from the word *apkros*, which means foam in Greek, and she was generally believed to have sprung from the foam.

Her first home was Cythera and her second Cyprus, and she was long linked closely with both islands.

Aphrodite is sometimes associated with war, though more generally with Ares, the god of war, with whom she had several children including Harmonia. About Harmonia Robert Graves writes: 'Harmonia, is, at first sight, a strange name for a daughter borne by Aphrodite to Ares; but, then as now, more than usual affection and harmony prevailed in a state which was at war.'*

Roman name: Venus

Ares

Ares was god of war, the only child Zeus and Hera had together. He revelled in fighting for its own sake and was constantly provoking men to battle, during which he would go from one side to the other, provoking and inciting.

He was once indicted for murder, the defendant in the first ever murder trial. It was said that he had killed a son of Poseidon, but Ares claimed that it was only to save his daughter Alcippe from rape. As there were no witnesses except Alcippe herself, who stoutly defended her father's word, the case was dismissed.

Roman name: Mars

Hermes

A son of Zeus by Maia, herself a daughter of Atlas, Hermes was born in Arcadia. He was associated with cunning and mischief, but was rarely malicious.

It was Hermes who invented the lyre and gave it to Apollo in exchange for some cows which Hermes had stolen and eaten.

Zeus used him as his messenger and Hermes is generally portrayed in this role wearing his winged sandals and hat and carrying his magic wand, the *Caduceus*, traditionally hung with white ribbons.

Hermes was eternally young, carefree and enchanting.

Roman name: Mercury

Hephaestus

Hera was so angry when she learned that Zeus had brought forth Athene that she resolved to have a child alone too. But unfortunately when born the child was so ugly that she regretted her decision and threw newly-born Hephaestus down from Olympus.

However, he was lucky enough to fall into the sea and was there rescued and cared for by Thetis and Eurynome, goddesses of the sea who were of a great deal kinder temperament than Hera.

Hephaestus grew up to be extremely skilled as a smith, and because of his talents, eventually found himself back in Olympus.

* Robert Graves *The Greek Myths* Vol. 1. (Penguin).

His wife was Aphrodite, who constantly cuckolded him, though he continued to love her and forgive her.

Hephaestus was an extremely popular god with the Greeks, and was very much respected for his kindly nature. Along with Athene he was patron of arts and crafts, and it was Hephaestus who was god of Fire.

Roman name: Vulcan

Dionysus

The worship of Demeter contained in the Eleusian Mysteries was later extended to include Dionysus too. As god of the vine he took his place beside the goddess of the corn, though she took slight precedence over him.

Not originally one of the twelve Olympians he joined them only after Hestia resigned her place to him.

Dionysus was a son of Zeus and of the mortal Semele; the only god who had a mortal parent.

He is constantly portrayed followed by a group of merry-makers, some human, some divine.

Like the Meanads who trailed after Dionysus, later followers tried to become possessed by him through excesses of wine and dancing and, sometimes, wild sacrifices in which the victim would be torn apart, as happened to Orpheus.

Roman name: Bacchus

Pan

Pan was never one of the Olympian Twelve, but nevertheless played an extremely important part in Greek mythology and was widely known and well liked by the Greeks.

He was usually believed to be a son of Hermes, although some said that he was a son of Penelope, fathered by all the men with whom she made love during Odysseus's twenty years' absence.

His appearance was, like that of the satyrs, half man and half goat, and he felt his lack of beauty very keenly though this never interfered with his pursuit of love with either sex.

Pan was the patron of shepherds and made his home in Arcadia, preferring the company of the Arcadians to that of the Olympians.

One delightful story which shows poor Pan in a rather ridiculous light also concerns Heracles, the great hero.*

After his twelve great labours were completed Heracles still continued to roam and was in fact sold as a slave for one year to

* Sometimes called Hercules, his Roman name.

Omphale, Queen of Lydia. The queen treated him very kindly, as she wanted him not as a worker but as her lover, which Heracles quickly became.

The couple did nothing but enjoy each other and Heracles ceased altogether to practise his manly sports, even going so far as to wear Omphale's clothes, while she would strut about in his lion's pelt, holding up his club and grimacing fearfully to the amusement of them both.

But Pan too loved Omphale and was determined to make love to her. One night Heracles and the lady went to spend a night in a shelter on a mountain top and after their usual games, exchanging clothes and so forth, went to sleep. However, what they did not expect or suspect was that Pan was hiding in the bushes nearby waiting until Heracles had time to fall asleep before approaching Omphale's couch.

When he was satisfied that all was quiet, and could wait no longer, Pan crept forward, through the darkness, to the shimmer of silk that he was sure covered Omphale's graceful form.

Stealthily lifting up the sheet at the end of the couch Pan crept under it, wriggling his way in to the bed with tender whispers and soft caresses. But Heracles – for it was Heracles of course, dressed in Omphale's best – woke up to find Pan in the bed and with a tremendous shout, kicked him out.

Heracles' monstrously loud voice woke Omphale immediately who joined Heracles in his laughter and jeering at an embarrassed and wretched Pan, sitting humiliated in the corner of their rough shelter.

But Pan had some revenge at least, for it was he who spread the story about Heracles' extremely odd habits of dress.

Roman name: Pan

Persephone

A daughter of Zeus and Demeter, Persephone became the wife of Hades and queen of the underworld, though only with the greatest reluctance.

As a young girl Persephone was playing with her companions when she was startled by Hades who caught her and took her with him down to Tartarus. He had been so swift and so sly that no one knew where she had gone and Demeter her mother wandered the earth, weeping and crying as she searched for Persephone.

In fact Demeter was so distracted by her grief that no crops grew because Demeter failed to dispense the gifts that were necessary. The men and women of Greece grew very alarmed as they faced starvation and Zeus realised that he must intervene.

So Zeus told Demeter where their daughter was, and said that Persephone could leave the Underworld. However as Persephone had already eaten the seeds of a pomegranate she was obliged to spend six months of every year with her husband.

Persephone's return to earth marks the beginning of Spring; her return to Hades marks the beginning of Winter.

Roman name: Proserpina

Eros

Although last in this list of gods and goddesses Eros is by no means least important. In fact some learned men felt that before Eros – whose name means sexual passion – there could have been no other life and that in the very beginning of time the goddess Night was courted and won by the Wind and that from this mating she laid a silver egg in the womb of Darkness and out of this egg hatched Eros, golden-winged and of both sexes. He then lived in a cave with Night, who was herself a trinity of Night, Order and Justice.

Before the cave sat Rhea, the mother, and inside the cave Eros created the earth, the sky, the sun and the moon which were ruled by the triple-goddess, Night.

More generally, however, Eros is portrayed as Aphrodite's son who was fathered perhaps by Ares, or Hermes, or even by Zeus himself.

He was regarded as irresponsible, too irresponsible in fact to join the Olympian Twelve, for he used his capability of making people fall in love quite recklessly, shooting arrows into their hearts indiscriminately. This did however once backfire on him somewhat, for sent by Aphrodite to shoot an arrow into the heart of a girl called Psyche, Eros misfired and the arrow went into his own heart and he fell desperately in love.

Fortunately Psyche (whose name means soul) returned his affections but trouble began when she wanted to see him, for no mortal could see a god and live. But finally Eros had to agree.

However the love that this couple had for each other was so obvious to the gods, and their separation so painful, that eventually they were reunited in Heaven where Zeus made Psyche immortal by feeding her some ambrosia, food of the gods, and Love and Soul were united for ever.

Roman name: Cupid

GODS OF THE SEA

Oceanus. Homer tells us that all gods and living creatures originated in the stream of Oceanus which encircles the world. He is more properly called a god of the water than god of the Sea for the early Greeks believed that from this encircling river came all the rivers and 'waters which gushed from the earth'. A Titan, Oceanus may be a son of Uranus and Gaea (Heaven and Mother Earth), and his might and power are exceedingly great.

A story which illustrated Oceanus's vulnerability, however, also concerns Heracles who was embarking on his tenth Labour and crossing between Europe and Africa. Heracles wished to make a strait there (if he *was* successful, this is the Strait of Gibraltar) and was sweating and straining as he tried to push the continents apart. Helius (the sun) was very interested in what Heracles was doing, and came closer to watch, but the nearer he went to Heracles the more unbearable the heat, and finally Heracles lost his temper completely and sent an arrow towards Helius. The sun god withdrew at once, his feelings hurt. But Heracles was so obviously sorry that Helius not only forgave him but also presented him with a golden goblet, shaped like a water-lily, in which Heracles could sail.

Oceanus however was not prepared to help Heracles and rocked the goblet violently, threatening to capsize Heracles. Again the hero lost his temper and again he seized his bow and arrow, threatening to shoot at Oceanus, who was so alarmed that he calmed the waves at once, and never troubled Heracles again.

Oceanus was married to his sister Tethys. Together they bore three thousand Oceanids, the nymphs of the great river that was Oceanus, and three thousand sons, gods of each of the rivers on earth. They are also said to have cared for the goddess Hera, Zeus's wife.

Pontus. His name means the Deep Sea, and Pontus was the oldest god of the waters, a son of Mother Earth born at the beginning of time. Nothing is known of him except his name and the fact that he is credited with the paternity of Nereus, a far more important god.

Nereus. This god was a son of Pontus and Mother Earth (Pontus's own mother). He is often called 'the Old Man of the Sea' – referring of course to the Mediterranean, though his name actually means 'wet one'. Nereus was gifted with the art of prophecy; Paris once saw him emerge from the waves and predict (accurately) the downfall of Troy. He was also able to change his shape at will, but like the other divinities of the sea, (with the exception of Poseidon, lord of the sea) he was reluctant to be seen or to speak.

Nereus was unfailingly kind and helpful, leaving his home only to assist sailors in trouble.

His wife was Doris, a nymph, and they lived together in the Aegean Sea. Together they had fifty daughters, called Nereids. The Nereids were mermaids with long golden hair, who shared their father's sweet nature, and waited on the Sea-goddess, Thetis, a sister Nereid.

Thetis. Thetis was so exceptionally beautiful that both Poseidon and Zeus wished to marry her. However it was predicted that if she was to have a son he would be greater than his father, and so both the gods withdrew their offers, and married her to Peleus, a great hero, but a mortal. Thetis was deeply offended at their choice, and tried hard to escape Peleus's advances by metamorphosing herself into a number of slippery shapes; but Peleus hung on and eventually she was won over by his ardour. Together they had several children, but the only one who grew to manhood was Achilles, who *was* even greater than his father. It was Thetis and her sister Eurynome who took Hephaestus into their underwater home when, newly-born and ugly, he had been so heartlessly thrown from Heaven by his mother Hera.

Phorcys. Phorcys was yet another son of Mother Earth and Pontus. Homer has said that he was the old man who ruled the waves, but little is known of him except that together with his sister Ceto he had several monstrous children, the Phorcids. These included Ladon, a dragon with a hundred heads who could speak with many tongues and who was to guard Hera's golden apple-tree; Echidne, (who was to marry Typhon and produce *more* monsters including the three-headed Hound of Hell, Cerberus and the Chimaera); the three Gorgons; the Graea and some say, the Hesperides (although Atlas is also credited with the paternity of the latter, as is Night).

The Hesperides also guarded the golden apple-tree given to Hera on her wedding night by Mother Earth, and it is generally assumed that Hera sent Ladon to guard the guardians, for she suspected the Hesperides of stealing the beautiful apples.

The Graea, whose name means literally the 'grey ones', were all born with grey hair. They were as graceful as swans, but had only one eye between them which they would pass from sister to sister.

The Gorgons were born beautiful but after one of them (Medusa) had profaned Athene's temple by making love in it with Poseidon, all three sisters were transformed into grotesque creatures so hideous in appearance that one glance at their faces would turn a man into stone. (See the story of Perseus and Medusa.)

Because of the hideous nature of his offspring, Phorcys was often associated with the stormy and cruel face of the sea.

Proteus. Thetis and Oceanus were Proteus's parents. He too was able both to prophesy and to change his shape, and he used the latter gift at will to try to evade exercising the former.

Proteus's only duty was to guard Poseidon's seals, though he would take a rest in a cave at midday, and then the seals would gather around and guard him.

Palaemon. Athamas, ruler of Boetia and brother of Sisyphus the cunning founder of Corinth, fell in love with Ino, daughter of Cadmus, founder of Thebes. Athamas was already married, but he put his first wife aside, married Ino and then allowed her to connive at a situation which led to the attempted sacrifice of Phrixus, Athamas's legal heir. (See the story of Jason and the Argonauts.) After the failure of this attempt Hera drove Athamas mad, not only because of his insult to Nephele, his first wife, (a phantom created by Zeus in the likeness of Hera) but also because Ino had with her in the palace Dionysus, the son of Zeus and Ino's sister Semele, a child whom she dressed as a girl to protect, unsuccessfully, from Hera.

Athamas in his madness killed one of the sons born to him and Ino and would have killed the other, and even Ino herself, but Ino gathered the younger child in her arms and ran to the shore,

leapt into the sea, and drowned them both. Because of the kindness she had shown to his son Dionysus however, Zeus made Ino
a goddess and the child, Palaemon, was also deified and sent to
the Isthmus of Corinth riding on the back of a dolphin.

Poseidon. Most important of all, this great Olympian was the
Lord and Ruler of the Mediterranean, the Friendly Sea (the
Black Sea) and of all underground rivers.

His story is fully told elsewhere in this book, as is the story of
Glaucus of Delos.

THE NAMING OF THE MYRTOAN SEA

Hippodameia was an exceptionally beautiful princess, a daughter of King Oenomaus, ruler of Pisa and Elis and a son of Ares, god of war.

Oenomaus was extremely fond of his daughter, many said so fond that he could not bear the thought of her belonging to another man, and so he devised a test for her many suitors which inevitably resulted in their death.

This test was to compete with the king himself in a chariot race, along a long course running from Pisa to the Isthmus of Corinth. This sounded reasonable enough, for all well-born men were adept at chariot racing, but Oenomaus had an unfair advantage for he raced with horses given to him by Ares his father. These horses had been conceived by the wind and could run just as fast, and no mere mortal horse could possibly compete, despite the half hour lead that Oenomaus inevitably gave.

Oenomaus did not drive the chariot himself, though he rode in it, but left the driving to Myrtilus, a son of Hermes who was himself desperately in love with Hippodameia, though he dared not risk competing for her.

A dozen or so men had already died in their pursuit of her hand, and the heads nailed above the gates of the city, when Pelops decided that he would make Hippodameia his bride.

Pelops was a son of Tantalus, a man who had been especially favoured by the gods but who had replied to their kindness by serving them a stew in which floated small pieces of his chopped up son, Pelops. The gods had quickly realised what they were being asked to eat, and in anger and disgust punished Tantalus and restored Pelops to life. Only Demeter, distracted by the loss of Persephone, had eaten a small morsel, a little piece of shoulder, but this was replaced by ivory.

It was somewhat daunting for Pelops to arrive at Pisa and find the heads of his fellow-competitors perched sightless on the city gates, but confident of the gods' protection he went to Oenomaus and offered himself as a competitor. He managed too to find a way to meet the girl herself, and though this had begun as a political scheme, he quickly fell in love with her, and she with him.

Pelops knew that alone he would have great difficulty in finding a way to beat Oenomaus, but with the aid of a fellow-conspirator he might have a chance.

Pelops had quickly decided that Myrtilus was his greatest hope, for he thought that he could exploit the charioteer's weakness for Hippodameia. So Pelops went to him with the proposition that if Myrtilus were to replace the lynch-pins in the axles of Oenomaus's chariot with similar pins made from wax, then Pelops would step aside and allow Myrtilus to spend the wedding night with the bride.

The thought of a night with Hippodameia so charmed Myrtilus that he readily agreed and carried out his side of the bargain as promised.

When the day of the race came Oenomaus and Myrtilus entered their chariot and beside Pelops rode Hippodameia, placed there by her father in an attempt to distract Pelops from the course.

The race began, with Pelops half an hour ahead, driving winged horses given to him by Poseidon, his special protector.

Then Oenomaus set off, spurring his immortal horses on at a terrifying speed but as they ran and the wheels turned, the wax lynch pins grew hotter and hotter until finally they melted, just at the point when Oenomaus was raising his magic spear, also given to him by Ares, to hurtle into Pelops's back.

The wheels of the chariot flew off and Oenomaus was thrown to the ground, and dragged along by his horses until he died, cursing Myrtilus and praying aloud that he in his turn would die at the hand of Pelops.

Eager now to see the bargain fulfilled, Myrtilus set off with Pelops and Hippodameia in their chariot which, drawn by Poseidon's winged horses, could travel over sea as well as land. The three eventually came to rest on a small island near Euboea, and then while Pelops went to fetch some water, Myrtilus approached Hippodameia, confident that now was the time to make love to her.

But Hippodameia cried out with alarm when he touched her and Pelops returned to find her struggling with poor confused Myrtilus. Offering no explanation of his bargain with Myrtilus

2

Pelops comforted the girl and all three returned to the chariot, to set off once more.

As they turned again over the sea Pelops suddenly and roughly pushed Myrtilus out of the chariot, throwing him down into the sea below, near the southernmost point of Euboea, Geraestus.

Myrtilus tumbled and fell into the sea, cursing Pelops as he went, and drowned in the waters beneath the chariot, which raced on.

Hermes was furious at this insult to his son and honoured the boy by placing his image among the stars as the Charioteer. He also renamed the sea, which stretches from Euboea to the Aegean, the Myrtoan Sea in his memory.

THE NAMING OF THE AEGEAN SEA

One of the greatest Greek heroes is Theseus, a son of Aegeus, King of Athens, and Aethra of Troezen.

Theseus was conceived during a one night encounter, planned by neither party, but before his father left his mother in the morning he told her that he would place his sword and sandals under a hollow rock, and if the child she was carrying was a boy, that when he was strong enough to lift the rock he should be told who his father was, and sent to him.

Aethra promised, and in due course bore her son, Theseus.

He grew up to be strong, fearless and intelligent, and when he was sixteen his mother took him to the rock and told him the story of his paternity, and without strain or difficulty, the boy lifted the great rock and found the sword and sandals beneath it.

Theseus then set out to visit his father, travelling not by sea as his mother and grandfather wanted, but by land. He had many adventures, and by the time he reached Athens word had spread of his courage and sense of justice, and the king was anxiously awaiting his arrival, not suspecting that the boy was his son, but fearful that he would prove to be a formidable rival for the throne.

The king was now married to Medea, formerly Jason's wife. She shared her husband's fears of a threat to the throne and suggested to him that they give the stranger a cup of poison to drink when he came to the palace to meet them.

Into Athens Theseus strode, greeted on all sides with cheers and cries of welcome. Boldly he went to the palace, and was taken in to meet the king and queen. Medea, who was a witch, recognised him at once and saw him now as an even greater threat, perhaps taking precedence as heir over her own son. But saying nothing about who he was to her husband she merely drew his attention to the welcome of the crowd, and the danger of Theseus's great popularity.

The party sat down to eat, and Medea placed the cup of poison in front of Theseus. But as the boy bent to pick up the cup, Aegeus, his father, noticed the sword which Theseus had with him. At once he tore the cup from Theseus's hand and threw the poison on the floor where it burned and stained.

Theseus turned to Medea, guessing that the poison had been made by her, but as he pursued her she wrapped herself in a magic cloud and he could not reach her. But her days in Athens were now numbered, and Aegeus sent her and her son into exile.

The news of Theseus's real identity spread like wildfire and the people were delighted, for had they not already recognised him as a hero?

The only dampener which marred the rejoicing was the common knowledge that very soon another party of young Athenians, seven girls and seven young men, would shortly have to sail to Crete to wander helplessly through the Labyrinth until devoured by the Minotaur. This hideous creature, half man and half bull, was the result of Pasiphae's strange passion for Poseidon's bull. The full story is told in the section on Daedalus, the inventor who built the labyrinth in which the Minotaur was housed. The odds were hopeless and not one member of the previous two parties, sent every nine years, had returned.

The tribute was demanded in retribution for the death of Androgeus, a son of Minos who had been killed in Attica.

Theseus now loved the people of Athens and shared their distress at this hideous punishment, so he offered himself as one of the fourteen, saying that he would try, with the help of the gods, to kill the Minotaur and end this torment to the people.

Aegeus was horrified at Theseus's decision, for once having discovered his son, he had no wish to lose him immediately and despite Theseus's confidence, he felt that the boy's optimism was completely unjustified, and that he would never see him again.

However Theseus was determined, and finally Aegeus had to agree, but before Theseus sailed he asked him to promise that if the expedition was successful that the black flag which the ship carried on its mast would be taken down, and a white one hoisted in its place to signify their victory. Theseus kissed his father goodbye, and promised.

Just how Theseus succeeded is told in the story of Ariadne and Theseus, but back in Athens Aegeus knew nothing of what had passed and was in a state of torment waiting for his son to return.

Every day he went to the Acropolis to scan the sea and the sky for the longed-for white sail.

Weeks passed, and Aegeus's anxiety grew as he paced the Acropolis, back and forth. But finally there was a speck on the horizon. With his excitement growing he waited for its colour to become discernible and then to his horror realised that without any doubt, the sail was black.

Whether Theseus simply forgot to change the sail, or whether he forgot his promise is not clear. But poor distraught Aegeus took it as a sign that his worst fears were confirmed. Theseus, he thought, must be dead. So no longer wishing to live, he threw himself into the sea and drowned.

From that time on, the sea was named the Aegean in his honour.

THE IONIAN SEA

The story of Io, after whom the Ionian Sea was named, is one of the most poignant in Greek Mythology and emphasises, perhaps more than any other, the lengths to which Hera would go to display her jealousy of Zeus's attentions to others.

Io was a daughter of the river-god Inachus, and a priestess of Hera. Zeus fell in love with her, perhaps unwittingly, for some say that he himself was a victim of Iynx, a daughter of Pan and Echo, and that Iynx had cast a spell over him.

Thinking that he would protect Io from Hera's revenge and spite, Zeus changed the girl into a beautiful white cow but when Hera discovered Zeus standing by the cow she was immediately suspicious and questioned him about the animal. Zeus swore that the cow had only then crossed his path and that he knew nothing about it, but Hera was not convinced and so asked Zeus if he would make her a present of the animal. Zeus was quite unable to refuse without revealing the truth and was forced to hand over the cow to Hera.

Io knew perfectly well what was going on for although she looked like a cow and was unable to speak, her feelings were still those of a girl, so it was in a state of great fear that she followed Hera to a meadow where she was to live. To ensure that the cow could not escape, and that Zeus could not visit her, Hera appointed as guard the watchman Argus who had a hundred eyes. Even when he slept he needed to close only a few of these eyes at a time, so was watching his helpless charge constantly.

Zeus knew that even Hermes, the fastest and most devious of thieves, would not be able to escape one of the many eyes of Argus, so instead Hermes charmed the watchman with his music and story-telling until finally, one by one, each of his eyes fell asleep. As soon as the hundredth eye closed Hermes cut off Argus's head, and released sad Io. Hera was enraged, and set the

eyes of her favourite watchman in the peacock's tail to remind
the world of his murder at the hand of Hermes. Then, before
Zeus could reach the cow, Hera sent a gadfly to torture her.

This gadfly buzzed around Io constantly, stinging her in the
tail and driving her near to madness. It seemed she would have no
escape for no matter where she went, the gadfly followed. First
Io went to Dodona, then reached the sea which is now called the
Ionian in her honour. But from this sea she turned back travelling
first North, then on to Asia Minor, Bactria and India. Then,
she wandered through Arabia to Ethiopia and then finally along
the Nile to Egypt where Zeus was finally able to restore her to her
human form. She then married Telegonus of Egypt but nevertheless bore a son to Zeus whom she named Epaphus, which means
'a touching'. Among her other descendants was Heracles, called
by many the greatest of all Greek heroes.

THE ISLES OF GREECE

THE isles of Greece! the isles of Greece
   Where burning Sappho loved and sung,
Where grew the arts of war and peace,
   Where Delos rose, and Phoebus sprung!
Eternal summer gilds them yet,
But all, except their sun, is set.

The Scian and the Teian muse,
   The hero's harp, the lover's lute,
Have found the fame your shores refuse:
   Their place of birth alone is mute
To sounds which echo further west
Than your sires' 'Islands of the Blest'.

The mountains look on Marathon –
   And Marathon looks on the sea;
And musing there an hour alone,
   I dreamed that Greece might still be free;
For standing on the Persians' grave,
I could not deem myself a slave.

A king sate on the rocky brow
   Which looks o'er sea-born Salamis;
And ships, by thousands, lay below,
   And men in nations; – all were his!
He counted them at break of day –
And when the sun set, where were they?

And where are they? and where art thou,
   My country? On thy voiceless shore
The heroic lay is tuneless now –
   The heroic bosom beats no more!
And must thy lyre, so long divine,
Degenerate into hands like mine?

'Tis something in the dearth of fame,
  Though linked among a fettered race,
To feel at least a patriot's shame,
  Even as I sing, suffuse my face;
For what is left the poet here?
For Greeks a blush – for Greece a tear.

Must *we* but weep o'er days more blest?
  Must *we* but blush? – Our fathers bled.
Earth! render back from out thy breast
  A remnant of our Spartan dead!
Of the three hundred grant but three,
To make a new Thermopylae!

What, silent still? and silent all?
  Ah! no; – the voices of the dead
Sound like a distant torrent's fall,
  And answer, 'Let one living head,
But one, arise, – we come, we come!'
'Tis but the living who are dumb.

In vain – in vain: strike other chords;
  Fill high the cup with Samian wine!
Leave battles to the Turkish hordes,
  And shed the blood of Scio's vine!
Hark! rising to the ignoble call –
How answers each bold Bacchanal!

You have the Pyrrhic dance as yet;
  Where is the Pyrrhic phalanx gone?
Of two such lessons, why forget
  The nobler and the manlier one?
You have the letters Cadmus gave –
Think ye he meant them for a slave?

Fill high the bowl with Samian wine!
  We will not think of themes like these!
It made Anacreon's song divine:
  He served – but served Polycrates –
A tyrant; but our master then
Were still, at least, our countrymen.

The tyrant of the Chersonese
  Was freedom's best and bravest friend;
That tyrant was Miltiades!
  O that the present hour would lend
Another despot of the kind!
Such chains as his were sure to bind.

Fill high the bowl with Samian wine!
  On Suli's rock, and Parga's shore,
Exists the remnant of a line
  Such as the Doric mothers bore:
And there, perhaps, some seed is sown,
The Heracleidan blood might own.

Trust not for freedom to the Franks –
  They have a king who buys and sells;
In native swords and native ranks
  The only hope of courage dwells:
But Turkish force and Latin fraud
Would break your shield, however broad.

Fill high the bowl with Samian wine!
  Our virgins dance beneath the shade –
I see their glorious black eyes shine;
  But gazing on each glowing maid,
My own the burning tear-drop laves,
To think such breasts must suckle slaves.

Place me on Sunium's marbled steep,
  Where nothing, save the waves and I,
May hear our mutual murmurs sweep;
  There, swan-like, let me sing and die:
A land of slaves shall ne'er be mine –
Dash down yon cup of Samian wine!

                    George Gordon Noel, Lord Byron

LEMNOS

Hephaestus, the Smith-god

Hephaestus, called both smith-god and god of fire, started life miserably for Hera his mother was so disappointed with his appearance at birth that she threw him down into the sea, where he would certainly have suffered greatly had he not been taken in by Thetis and Eurynome, two sea goddesses.

They kept him hidden in an underwater grotto for some years, and Hera forgot him. Then one day Thetis went up to Olympus wearing the most exquisitely made jewellery. Hera was at once curious to know where Thetis had got it, for she loved beautiful things and liked to possess more than any other goddess.

Thetis was very reluctant to tell her, for the jewellery had been made by none other than Hephaestus who designed and executed the lovely objects in gratitude for the kindness the sea goddesses had shown towards him. Hera cajoled and pleaded however, and finally Thetis had no choice but to tell her who the workman was.

At once Hera demanded that Hephaestus should leave his adopted home and be brought up to Olympus where she set up the most marvellous smithy in which he could work.

Hephaestus is always described as ill-tempered, but certainly he must have been a forgiving god too, for despite his mother's early rejection he did go back to Olympus and was soon busy trying to fulfil all the gods' and goddesses' many demands. His work has never been surpassed, and his creativity was such that he made some women from gold who could walk and talk and help him with his tasks, and a set of three-legged tables which could run on their golden wheels.

Whether or not Hephaestus was ever totally reconciled with Hera we do not know, but certainly when Zeus hung her from Heaven by her wrists as punishment for leading a short-lived rebellion against him, Hephaestus dared to reproach him for his conduct.

Zeus, who could never tolerate criticism of any sort, quickly retaliated by throwing poor Hephaestus down from Olympus for a second time. Down, down he fell for a whole day. When finally he landed it was on the island of Lemnos, and the impact was so great that he broke both his legs and when the islanders found him he was in a shaken and very poor condition. But despite his unfortunate experience, Lemnos remained Hephaestus's favourite island.

His services were too valuable for him to remain out of Olympus for long, so he returned, but the effects of the fall stayed with him and he could not walk again without golden leg-supports.

Where 'Burning Sappho' sang

Lesbos, which is also known by the name of its chief town Mytilene, has been made famous by the poems of Sappho, the greatest of women poets.

Sappho should not, strictly speaking, find a place in a book of Greek Mythology, but her association with the island of Lesbos has become legendary and believing that no visitor to the island, or lover of Greece, should remain unaware of her story, I have taken the liberty to give it the briefest of re-tellings, and to include one of her surviving poems.

To mythology purists I apologise, and suggest the turning of a page.

Sappho lived on Lesbos about 590 BC, a time when the island was a centre of world trade and communications and its capital, Mytilene, was among the most civilised and advanced cities of the world. A highly cultured intellectual life flourished and out of this congenial and stimulating atmosphere two great poets came forward. One, Alcaeus, is known only to scholars, but the name of the other has enjoyed much wider fame, though much of it of a nature that Sappho would surely least have sought.

Sappho wrote magnificent, tender, erotic poetry, addressed to girls, describing the effects of physical love in a way that has not been equalled since.

Later generations have usually described her as a lesbian, frequently as a term of derogation, and the very word is derived from her island home. But it seems – subjectively at least – far more likely that Sappho was a truely sensual woman, able to see and love beauty in both sexes. Certainly one story tells that she committed suicide for the love of a man, leaping from a cliff at Levkas in the Ionian Islands.

Her poems were thought by the Christian church to be of an

evil nature and in 1073 they were burned in Constantinople.
Fortunately for posterity many fragments survived.
Here is one of her songs.

Blest as the immortal gods is he
The youth who fondly sits by thee
And hears and sees thee all the while
Softly speak and sweetly smile.

'Twas this deprived my soul of rest
And raised such tumults in my breast;
For while I gazed, in transport tossed,
My breath was gone, my voice was lost:

My bosom glowed; the subtle flame
Ran quick through all my vital frame;
Over my dim eyes a darkness hung;
My ears with hollow murmurs rung.

In dewy damps my limbs were chilled;
My blood with gentle horror thrilled;
My feeble pulse forgot to play;
I fainted, sank, and died away.

(Tr. Phillip

The Death of Orpheus

In all Greek history there is no more famous poet and musici
than Orpheus. He was given his lyre by Apollo himself and h
as his music teachers the Muses. Trees, animals, birds would
listen to his playing and follow his commands.

When he was a young man Orpheus joined the Argonauts a
sailed with them to Colchis, then, on his return, he fell in lo
with a gentle and lovely girl named Eurydice whom he soo
married.

The young couple were exceptionally happy and revelled
each other's love. However one day as she walked alone in
valley Eurydice was approached by a young man who tried fir
to seduce her by clever words and flattery, and then to rape h
when she resisted him. In anger and fear Eurydice pulled hers

away, running from him blinded by tears and not seeing where she ran. Her carelessness proved to be very expensive for after taking only a few steps she trod on a venomous snake which immediately bit her, and she died.

Orpheus was inconsolable. He could not bear the thought of life without Eurydice and with great courage he went to Tartarus, the land of the dead, to try to bring his wife back.

With his singing and playing Orpheus was able to charm the ferryman Charon to take him across the River Styx which encircles the land of the dead. The fierce three-headed dog Cerberus and the three Judges of the dead were also deeply affected by these sounds. His lovely music soothed the suffering of the tortured souls and even Hades was so touched that he agreed to allow Eurydice to return with her husband to the land of the living. There was, however, one condition – Orpheus could lead Eurydice out, but was never once to look at her until they reached sunlight.

Orpheus willingly agreed to this condition, and the two set out with Orpheus leading the way and guiding Eurydice through the darkness with his joyful singing. But just as they saw a crack of light ahead Orpheus was struck by the thought that Eurydice might have been altered, deformed in some hideous way by her experiences and so horrified was he by this thought that he forgot Hades' warning and turned to look at Eurydice.

In that brief glance Orpheus saw that Eurydice had lost nothing of her beauty but that even in the second that he looked she was slipping away from him, back to the dark world of the dead.

Now Eurydice was lost for ever. Orpheus still made music but it was a much graver, more sombre music with a wistful quality which was strangely moving.

Orpheus found no other woman to take Eurydice's place, though some say that he turned to his own sex for consolation and by this offended Aphrodite. It was at this time too that Dionysus came to Thrace, and Orpheus found the excesses he advocated crude and disgusting and argued against them, thereby estranging Dionysus, though not the men of Thrace who listened to him carefully and took note of his arguments against the practices of Dionysus.

Gradually Dionysus's hate for Orpheus grew. He saw him as a stumbling block to the uninhibited following of Dionysian rites which included sacrifice, deplored by Orpheus. The Maenads who attended Dionysus echoed his anger and finally they struck. Waiting until all their husbands were with Orpheus in Apollo's temple they gathered together and marched to the temple and taking the weapons which had been left outside they forced an entry. The men inside were brutally murdered by their wine-maddened wives who when they finally reached Orpheus tore him to pieces, limb by limb.

The Muses, Orpheus's music teachers, were horrified and grief stricken at his barbaric death, and collected together his limbs and took them for burial to the foot of Mount Olympus, where the birds now sing more beautifully than anywhere else in the world.

Orpheus's magnificent head was thrown by the crazed Maenads into the River Hebrus which carried it, still singing, to the island of Lesbos. There it was placed in a cave where it continued not only to sing but to prophesy with such wisdom that people stopped going to Apollo's oracles at Delphi or Clarus or Gryneium. Eventually Apollo could bear this no longer and went to Lesbos where he ordered Orpheus to be silent, though later he placed an image of his Lyre in the sky to honour him.

Arion of Lesbos

Arion was a son of Poseidon and the nymph Onaea. He was extremely handsome and talented, especially at music, and played the lyre exquisitely.

Word of his playing spread and Arion was invited to Taenarus in Sicily to compete in a festival of music. He was at this time living in Corinth, under the protection of Periander who was extremely fond of him and valued his presence highly. When Arion told Periander of the invitation to Taenarus Periander's immediate reaction was to persuade Arion to refuse, but Arion was excited at the thought of exhibiting his talents to a new audience and begged and pleaded so effectively that finally Periander was forced to give his consent.

Arion made the journey to Taenarus without incident, and won every prize the festival offered. The ranks of his admirers swelled overnight and he was given many rich gifts as tokens of their esteem.

By the time Arion left Sicily he had accumulated a rare pile of treasures which did not escape the attention of the sailors who had been hired to sail him back to Corinth. When the ship was out of harbour and on the high sea the captain went to Arion and told him that unfortunately he would have to die as the riches he carried with him were worth more than his life and he, the Captain, and his crew intended to have them.

Arion tried to make a bargain with the captain, saying that he would give the sailors his treasure in return for his life. But the captain would not accept such a bargain, replying that Arion would later retract and deny that the exchange was a fair one. Arion had to die.

All seemed to be lost. The sea was empty for miles around and those on board were united in their greed and their anxiety to be rid of Arion. With a sweet, sad face, he turned to the captain and asked for permission to be allowed to sing just one last song before death.

This request was so harmless that the captain was happy to agree, so Arion dressed himself in his most beautiful clothes, stood straight on the pr w of the ship and sang a song to the gods, imploring their help in this desperate moment.

For several minutes the boy sang, in a voice filled with a passion that had never been sweeter. Then, without a look behind him, he leapt from the prow to the sea below. The ship sailed on while the crew argued and fought over the division of Arion's treasures.

But Arion's song had been heard, not only by the gods but also by a school of dolphins which was just then passing by the ship. They had gathered around the prow to hear the glorious music and when Arion leapt he found himself among them and immediately clambered onto the back of the dolphin nearest to him and was carried to the port of Corinth, with the other dolphins swimming at his side.

The gentle, gaceful dolphins were able to move through the water at a far greater speed than a ship, so Arion arrived in Corinth several days before the crew and ship he had so recently and ignominiously left. At once he raced to Periander to tell him the story of the treachery and with him he took the dolphin who had carried him so nobly on his back.

Periander was overwhelmingly grateful to the dolphin for having saved Arion's life and every attention of the court was showered upon it. But in their eagerness to please the dolphin its hosts quite forgot that the creature was used only to simple sea life, and after just a few days the dolphin died from overindulgence.

Soon the ship arrived in the port and Periander at once sent a messenger to summon the captain and crew to the court where he affected great anxiety over Arion's absence and asked the captain for news of his protege. The captain pulled a very long face and said that Arion had been unable to resist the flatterers of Taenarus and would not be persuaded to return home. He had tried, said the captain, but the boy would not listen to reason. Over the burial spot of the dead dolphin the sailors swore that their story was true.

Now Arion emerged from his hiding place and stood before his would-be murderers. In horror they recoiled from him, scarcely able to believe that he was real. Shaking and mumbling they could not excuse their guilt, so without delay they were taken away for execution.

When Arion died he was honoured by Apollo, patron of music, who placed his image among the stars where a boy with a lyre can still be seen.

CHIOS

Orion, the handsomest man alive

Orion was a son of Poseidon and acclaimed by all as the most handsome man alive.

This prince among men fell in love with Merope, the daughter of the King of Chios. The king's name was Oenopion and he was also well born being one of the sons of Dionysus and Ariadne.

To prove his love for Merope Orion undertook for Oenopion to clear the island of all wild beasts, for he took great pleasure in hunting.

However when Orion had killed all the animals on the island, and presented himself to claim Merope as his bride, the king refused to acknowledge his success saying that there were still beasts roaming the hills, because men could hear their calls.

Orion was furious, for he knew that this was not true, but Oenopion was adamant, the truth of the matter being that he himself was also in love with Merope and could not bear the thought of another man having his daughter as a bride.

For some time Orion was patient, but at last he could bear the waiting no longer. Having drunk a great deal of wine he broke into Merope's bedroom and took the girl by force. When Oenopion heard of this he called upon his father Dionysus to send satyrs, who gave Orion more and more wine to drink until he was quite unconscious.

Oenopion then dragged Orion to the seashore, poked out both his beautiful eyes, and left him on the beach.

When Orion finally woke from his drunken sleep and found himself in permanent darkness he was very, very frightened, but an oracle told him that if he went to the east and let the sun fall on his eyes, that he would then be able to see again.

Orion clumsily found his way to a boat and made the journey to Lemnos. There he enlisted the help of one of Hephaestus's young apprentices, a boy named Cedalion, and carrying him on his shoulders as a guide, Orion set out towards the east until he could go no further and had reached the point where Helius (the sun) begins his journey across the sky.

There Eos fell in love with Orion. She was Dawn, a daughter of the Titans, who announced the rising of her brother Helius, and his departure from the sky, with her rosy fingers and her saffron robe. She was generally liked by the gods but once Aphrodite found her in bed with Ares, the god of war and Aphrodite's own lover, and the goddess was so angry that she cursed gentle Eos with a great lust for young mortals; Orion was to be the first of many.

Eos now interceded with Helius on Orion's behalf, and the sun restored Orion's sight.

The very minute that Orion could see again he was determined to take his revenge on Oenopion for his suffering during the weeks of blackness and so with Eos at his side, Orion went back to Chios, stopping briefly at Delos, Apollo's birthplace, on the way.

But when the couple reached Chios the king was not to be found, for he had a secret underground room which had been built for him by Hephaestus, and was hiding there out of sight.

So Orion and Eos went on to Crete, for Orion suspected that Oenopion might have sought refuge with his grandfather, Minos. They did not of course find Oenopion on the island, but they did meet Artemis (sister of Apollo and goddess of hunting) who greeted them warmly, inviting Orion to forget his revenge and to join her in a hunt.

Apollo was not at all pleased when he saw that Artemis and Orion were hunting together, for he feared that Orion's beauty might have the same effect on Artemis (virgin goddess though she was) that it had obviously had on Eos, who had been so indiscreet as to make love with Orion on Apollo's own island (an event which even now makes Eos blush with shame). More than that, Apollo overheard Orion's boast that he was so fine a hunter that he could rid the whole earth of unwanted wild beasts.

With careful cunning Apollo went to Mother Earth, repeating to her Orion's immodest boast and inciting Mother Earth to send at once a snake in pursuit of Orion.

When he saw the snake approaching Orion sent one of his arrows flying towards its back, but to his amazement the arrow just bounced off, and the snake, unmoved, continued to crawl towards him. Orion then tried to defend himself with his sword but again found that it made no impression at all on the inviolable snake. Quickly realising that he was being pursued by a most uncommon creature, Orion ran to the sea and began to swim towards Delos hoping to reach Eos and gain her protection.

Apollo now went to Artemis, drawing her attention to the far-off swimmer and telling Artemis that it was a villain who had raped one of Artemis's priestesses. At once Artemis reacted, pulling an arrow from the quiver at her side, and with one well-aimed shot, killed Orion.

Now Artemis swam out to sea to claim her prize, but was of course horrified to find that the floating corpse was Orion. She turned to Asclepius, (Apollo's son, and god of healing), for help, asking him to restore Orion back to life. But before Asclepius could do so, Zeus struck him dead.

Unable to enjoy Orion alive, Artemis nevertheless ensured that he would live on in memory by placing his image in the sky where he continues to be chased by the snake.

SAMOS

Hera

Samos was a centre of worship of Hera, and a small part of the *Heraion*, or Sanctuary of Hera can still be seen on the coast of the island at a place called Kolonna. This was the largest Greek Temple ever built, one of the seven wonders of the world, and those that believed that Hera was born on Samos (Argos was another favoured site) say that the spot was chosen for its proximity to the torrent Imbrasos which witnessed her birth.

Hera, wife of Zeus, was also his sister and a child of Cronus and Rhea. She was their second-born and like her elder sisters Hestia and Demeter, and those that came after them, Hades and Poseidon, she was swallowed by her father Cronus. However the experience seems to have done them little harm for when Zeus rescued them they came out of their father's stomach fully grown and thoroughly militant.

Zeus wooed Hera with great ardour, but she was not at all interested in him and tried to rebuke him. So the wily god changed himself into a pathetic little cuckoo which Hera held to her breast to protect. At once Zeus changed into his own shape again and took her by force, ensuring that she would marry him.

Zeus and Hera spent their wedding night on Samos, a wedding night which lasted for three hundred years.

RHODES

The Telchines

The Telchines were squat gnome-like creatures who were said to have the evil eye.

Their first home was on Rhodes, and they were probably that island's very earliest inhabitants. There were nine Telchines, each with a dog's head and flippers instead of hands. They were skilful doctors and smiths who used their talents not for good but for evil, maliciously ruining crops and interfering with the weather. It is the Telchines who are credited with having made the sickle which Cronus used when castrating Uranus.

Poseidon is thought to have been entrusted to their safekeeping when young by Mother Earth, and despite their rather unusual appearance to have fallen in love with one, Halia, with whom he shared the begetting of the nymph Rhode, who was to be wife to Helius. Poseidon and Halia also had six sons who inherited the worst of the Telchines' traits and even dared to obstruct Aphrodite when she was making her majestic way across the waves from Cythera, her first island home, to Cyprus, her second.

After founding the cities of Kameiros, Ialysos and Lindos these strange creatures left Rhodes to Rhode and her family and moved on to Crete where they were then that island's first inhabitants. But again they upset all weather expectations and made it impossible to grow successful crops and the Cretans grew very tired of them. Zeus too was angry at the effect they were having on his favourite island, so he resolved to get rid of them in a flood. But Artemis, the virgin huntress, took pity on them and told them of Zeus's plan. So they all left Crete, and scattered over different parts of Greece for safe-keeping.

*

Island of the Sun

Rhodes must hold a very special place in the affections of to-day's sun-worshippers, for it was this island which was given to Helius, the sun-god, as his own, and it was named after Rhode, his wife.

Helius was born from the Titan Hyperion and the Titaness Thea, as was his sister, Selene, the Moon.

It was his magnificent duty to make the daily journey in his chariot across the sky from his place in the East to the furthest point in the west (the Islands of the Blessed) where he plunged into the sea and was carried by Ocean in his golden goblet back to the eastern point so that he could again begin his route from the east in the morning.

It was generally thought that Helius's head was surrounded by the brilliant disk of the sun, and this is usually how he was portrayed. He drove four magnificent horses whose exotic names when translated meant Blazing, Fiery, Flaming and Orient.

Helius's journey is more readily understandable if it is understood that the early Greeks believed that the world was circle-shaped and flat except for the mountains and hills which protruded out of it. This world was capped by a dome (sometimes thought to be made of bronze or iron) and the sun and stars were seen to rise at one end of this dome, and to go down at the other. As they constantly rose in the same place it was assumed, logically enough, that they had to travel back to their starting point, presumably under the ground or along the Ocean, the great stream which flowed in a circle marking the boundary of the plain they thought of as earth.

When Zeus was allocating lands and cities to the gods he quite forgot to include Helius, and it was not until everything had been shared out that Zeus suddenly realised his grave omission.

Many of the gods would have been bitterly offended at this oversight, but Helius had a most generous nature and was co-operative enough to tell Zeus that in his travels (for Helius was all-seeing) he had noticed a new island beginning to emerge which may, perhaps, have been an old island buried since the great flood. This was the land he wanted.

Zeus was delighted to have a delicate problem solved and only too willing to agree that as soon as the island had completely emerged that it should be Helius's own.

Helius was married to the Nymph Rhode, daughter of Poseidon and Helia the Telchine, with whom he had eight children. Out of love and respect for his wife, Helius named their new home in her honour.

The sons of Rhode and Helius were famed as astronomers; their sister Electryo was renowned for her piety and virginity and became a demi-goddess. One of the brothers was banished from the island after committing fratricide and went to Egypt where he named a city Heliopolis in honour of his father, and became the first man to teach the Egyptians astronomy.

Three towns on Rhodes – Ialysos, Kamiros and Lindos – are named in honour of Rhode's grandsons.

Phaëthon Drives the Chariot of the Sun

Phaëthon was the result of a passionate love affair between Helius, the Sun, and Clymene, a lady with many husbands and even more lovers who is said to have come from the east.

Until the child was eight or nine, or thereabouts, he lived only with his mother, and though Clymene frequently pointed to the Sun as he travelled across the sky, telling Phaëthon that it was his father, the child felt troubled and insecure, especially when his school mates teased him about not having a father at home.

Finally Clymene knew that Phaëthon should actually go to the Sun, to be acknowledged by his father; and then, she thought, he would be happy again.

So Phaëthon travelled as far east as it was possible to go and there reached the palace of Helius which glittered and shone magnificently with the most rare and splendid stones which were studded all over the great walls.

With mounting excitement Phaëthon approached the palace, and walked into the presence of the Sun who at once recognised him and welcomed him with great affection.

To celebrate Phaëthon's arrival Helius promised the boy that he could have any gift that he wanted. Phaëthon thought for the briefest of seconds, and then, without any hesitation, told the Sun that he would like to drive his chariot across the sky. Once, just once, he pleaded as he saw Helius's face grow stern. The boy vividly remembered the awe and amazement he had felt every time his mother had pointed out Helius making his way grandly across the sky, and Phaëthon thought how marvellous it would be to inspire such feelings, even if it was to be for only one glorious time.

But Helius knew what danger such a journey would be for Phaëthon and tried again and again to dissuade him, telling him of the great perils involved in that seemingly smooth journey across the sky. Phaëthon could have anything, Helius told him, but to drive the chariot was madness. But Phaëthon insisted, and because he had promised him that his wish would be fulfilled, Helius had to agree, though he did so with the greatest misgivings.

In his excitement however Phaëthon refused to notice the obvious anxiety of his father and instead concentrated all his energy and attention on the treat that lay ahead.

Gravely Helius tried to warn him of the perils of the course. Phaëthon would have to take the chariot up from the sea on a path steeper than any other. When he reached the highest point of his course at midday he would be at such a distance from the ground that it would make him giddy to look down, and when the time came to make the descent to the west the way would be so precipitous that daily the sea-gods held their breath as Helius brought the chariot back down towards the ocean.

Phaëthon barely listened to his father, and when Helius went on to warn him that even the creatures in the constellations – the Lion, the Crab, the Scorpion, the Bull – would reach out to try to distract and harm him, Phaëthon merely laughed, seeing nothing ahead but the glory that would be his as he rode proudly across the sky.

As the night drew to a close Helius talked to his son, but his words fell on deaf ears and when the gates of the east were suffused with a purple light he knew that he had to let his son go.

The courts of Dawn filled with Light, warm and rosy; the stars were already disappearing. The horses who could fly faster than the East Wind were bridled and ready, and Phaëthon climbed into the chariot behind them, took the reins into his hands, and they were away, without even a second to shout goodbye.

Up and up the chariot went, and Phaëthon was elated. It was every bit as exciting and thrilling as he had hoped. But suddenly the horses realised that they were being guided not by the sure, firm hand of Helius, but by a strange and weak creature who could never control them. Now they were free! At once the beasts left their usual path and galloped madly through the sky. Phaëthon's excitement fast turned into fear, and though he tried to bring some order to his driving he knew at once that he had no chance of matching his feeble strength against that of the freedom-struck horses.

Shaking and crying with terror Phaëthon hung on grimly as the horses made their way higher and higher, further and further from earth until the people below were no longer able to feel the heat of the sun and trembled and shivered with cold. Then, suddenly, at breakneck speed, the horses turned and raced towards earth where the great heat of the sun burned first the mountain tops and then the fields and the people's shivering changed to trepidation as they faced the threat of being burnt alive.

Phaëthon could bear no more. Choking with smoke, and trembling with shame, his fear was so great that he only wished to die. Mother Earth, who had watched these awful events with increasing anxiety, was able to bear the destruction he was bringing no longer and cried out to the gods for help. With his thunderbolt, a now angered Zeus struck Phaëthon dead, the chariot shattered and the crazed horses plunged headlong into the sea.

The burning body of Phaëthon fell into the River Eridanus – which no mortal has ever seen – and there the water quenched the flames and soothed his body which was later gently buried by the naiads. His sisters came to the river bank to mourn him and were so struck by grief that they turned into poplar trees.

The story of Althaemenes

Althaemenes was a son of Catreus, king of Crete and the eldest surviving son of Minos.

Catreus had several children, but Althaemenes was his only son and when it was predicted that one of his children would kill Catreus, Althaemenes and his sister, Apemosyne, left Crete for Rhodes believing that they were diminishing the chances of the prediction coming true.

Together they founded the city of Cretinia (*Kretinae*) and later Althaemenes founded Cameirus (*Kameiros*) alone. From the highest point of the island he could look across on a clear day and see his beloved Crete.

The inhabitants of Rhodes liked Althaemenes very much, perhaps because he built an altar to Zeus and set around it bronze bulls which would roar a warning if Rhodes was threatened.

Althaemenes was not however a kind man, and when his sister Apemosyne came running to him to tell how Apollo had pursued her until she slipped and fell, and that he had then raped her, Althaemenes refused to believe her, and in anger and disgust killed her with a violent kick.

Time passed on Crete. Catreus's other daughters married, and one became the mother of Agamemnon* and Menelaus. Eventually Catreus was quite alone, and despairing of ever seeing his beloved son again, he set out to Rhodes to visit Althaemenes.

On a dark moonless night Catreus and his men arrived on Rhodes, but their shouts of identification could not be heard as the dogs on the island were barking so loudly. Eager to defend Rhodes, Althaemenes ran forward thinking that the invaders were pirates; and failing to recognise his father in the dark, Althaemenes ran a spear through Catreus, killing him instantly.

The morning light revealed what he had done. Despite Althaemenes' self-imposed exile, the oracle's prediction had come true and Catreus had died at the hand of one of his children, his only beloved son.

With a great cry of anguish Althaemenes prayed aloud for the earth to swallow him up, and as he prayed a chasm appeared at his feet and Althaemenes fell into it, disappearing from sight.

* Agamemnon's story is told in LAND OF ZEUS. His brother, Menelaus, was Helen of Troy's legal husband.

First Home of Zeus

While Rhea was expecting Zeus, her sixth child by Cronus, she determined that the unborn child would escape the fate of his older brothers and sisters who had all been swallowed by Cronus who feared the realisation of a prediction that he would be usurped by a son, just as his father had been by Cronus himself.

So when the time came for her to give birth, Rhea stole away under the shroud of night to Arcadia where Zeus was born. She then passed the baby to her mother, Mother Earth, and went back to Olympus where she gave the unsuspecting Cronus a stone wrapped in swaddling clothes and approximating in size to a newly-born god. Cronus accepted this and swallowed it, relieved at having once more evaded the threat.

Meanwhile Mother Earth took the baby to Crete and hid him in the cave of Dicte on the Aegean Hill.

There Zeus was cared for by two gentle nymphs who fed him milk from a goat, and sweet honey. This sustained him so well that when Zeus later became Lord of the Sky he placed the goat's image in the sky to be honoured as Capricorn and took one of her horns to become the famous horn of plenty – the Cornucopia. This was always filled with whatever the user most wanted, whether food or drink, and it too was later placed among the stars as an emblem of plenty.

In order that Cronus should not find the baby either on earth, or on the sea or in the heavens, his cradle was hung from a tree.

Around the cradle stood the Curetes, guardians who ensured that Cronus could not hear Zeus's cries. By banging their spears against their shields, they created the most incredible din that would have drowned a thousand babies' cries.

Eventually however Cronus became suspicious and pursued Zeus and his faithful nurses, but Zeus was able to evade him by turning himself into a serpent and the nurses into bears, remembered in yet another constellation.

Today's visitors to Crete may visit Zeus's cave, the Diktaean Cave, which was excavated at the end of the 19th Century.

Zeus abducts Europa

Europa was the charming and very beautiful daughter of Aegnor and Telephassa, and sister of Cadmus (founder of Thebes), Cilix, Phineus, Phoenix and Thasus.

Her innocence and gaiety caught Zeus's eye and never one to try to allay his passions, he planned to abduct and seduce her. Zeus's problems were however twofold for not only had he to find a way to carry the girl off, but he also had to avoid Hera's keen and ever-watchful eye. So the god hit upon the plan of transforming himself into a bull.

> The gods themselves,
> Humbling their deities to love, have taken
> The shapes of beasts upon them. Jupiter
> became a bull, and bellow'd.
>
> Shakespeare.

Hermes was sent to drive Aegnor's cattle by the sea, in the place where Europa and her companions played, and Zeus joined them. Europa was at once drawn to the beautiful bull and put her arms around his neck, crying out to her friends to see how charming he was and how warm and tender his eyes.

The girls placed flowers around his neck and soon became so fond of the bull and so unafraid that Europa climbed upon his back, at which point Zeus turned towards the sea and raced off with Europa clinging for her life to his horns. Her startled friends could do nothing to help Europa who was by now terrified, and crying desperately for help. But Zeus raced on over the sea riding the waves until the girl and bull had disappeared from the sight of Europa's startled companions left far behind.

Zeus and Europa travelled on until they reached Crete, and there Zeus ran onto the shore into a thicket. Europa fell off his back and Zeus at once changed himself into an eagle and made love to her.

Europa bore Zeus three sons, Minos, Rhadamanthys and Sarpendon.

After the birth of her sons, Europa married the king of Crete, a man named Asterius. The couple had no children so Asterius named Europa and Zeus's sons as his heirs, but when they grew up the brothers quarrelled over a beautiful boy, a son of Apollo. Eventually the boy decided that he loved Sarpendon best and left Crete with him for Asia Minor.

When Asterius died it was Minos who succeeded him, and Rhadamanthys, who had remained in Crete, lived peaceably alongside his more assertive brother.

Who was King Minos?

King Minos was the son of Zeus and Europa, the beautiful girl Zeus abducted and took across the waters to Crete.

There is a tradition that he was a great lawmaker and founder of the first great naval power. Certainly he gave his name to the Minoan Culture and Minos may well have been the royal title of successive kings.

The Minos of legend ruled Crete with Pasiphaë, a daughter of Helius the sun-god and the nymph Crete, who may well have given her name to the island. Their children were Catreus, Ariadne, Glaucus and Phaedra. Another daughter, Acacallis, was said to be Apollo's first love, though when the girl told Minos that she had been seduced by the god he was so displeased that he banished her to Libya.

Offspring of Minos were also found on the island of Paros. Their mother was the nymph Paria, and the island was named in her honour.

After Minos's death Zeus wished to honour him, and his brother Rhadamanthys, by making them immortal, but the other gods felt that this would create a dangerous precedent (as many of them had fathered children with mortals) so Zeus conceded and instead appointed them Judges of the Dead.

The Minoan period is the Cretan Bronze Age divided into three main periods stretching from circa 3000 – 1100 BC.

Our knowledge of it is in the main due to the two great men, Heinrich Schliemann and Arthur Evans. It was Schliemann who master-minded the excavations of Troy, Mycenae and Tiryns, and Evans who carried on the research and ten years after Schliemann's death began in 1900 to excavate the *Knossos*, the Minoan capital with its great palace and surrounding buildings and cemetries, which must surely rank as one of the world's most spectacular archeological finds.

Visitors to Crete may visit parts of the Knossos and also the Herakleion Museum which contains finds from the Minoan Age. This cannot be too highly recommended but it might be as well to do some preliminary reading to make the visits more intelligible. I would suggest Leonard Cottrell's *The Bull of Minos* (Evans Bros.) which gives the reader a wealth of facts in a clear and constantly fascinating way.

Daedalus, the great inventor

There lived and flourished long ago, in famous Athens town,
One Daedalus, a carpenter of genius and renown;
('Twas he who with an augur taught mechanics how to bore, —
An art which philosophers monopolised before.)

Saxe.

Daedalus would never have left Athens and gone to Crete if he had not been overcome by jealousy, though it was not jealousy over a woman, but rather over a young boy which drove him away.

Daedalus was renowned for his skills as an inventor, an architect and as a smith. He had a number of apprentices with him at all times, and when his sister Polycaste asked if her son Talos, could join him, Daedalus was happy to agree.

Quickly however it became obvious to Daedalus that Talos was quite unusually talented and that even at the age of twelve he would quickly become a formidable competitor. One day Talos found the spine of a fish which he used to saw a stick in half He then made a replica in iron of the fish's spine and in this way the first saw was made. Then as if this was not enough he added the potter's wheel and a compass to his list of inventions and the people of Athens became very excited, exclaiming about his cleverness and ignoring Daedalus completely.

Daedalus could not bear the situation to continue, so he enticed the innocent boy to the top of the Acropolis and then drew him near as though to point out distant landmarks. But as the boy stood trustingly beside him, Daedalus gave him a hearty push, and Talos fell to his death.

Quickly Daedalus ran to the foot of the Acropolis and tried to stuff the broken corpse into a large bag he had brought for the purpose. But his activities aroused the curiosity of passers-by who were not satisfied with his explanation that it was a serpent he was putting in the bag. Soon Daedalus was brought to trial, and banished from Athens.

Daedalus now found his way to Crete, and King Minos was delighted to receive him knowing that he could use his services and the fact that Daedalus was a murderer did not affect his welcome at all.

Life went well for Daedalus in Crete. He had a son with one of Minos' slave girls, and named him Icarus, and spent his time making delightful carved dolls for the family.

Pasiphaë, the Cretan Queen, had also taken a liking to Daedalus and confided in him her passion for the bull which had come up to Crete from the sea. It had arrived at the time when Minos was making his claim to the throne of Crete, and to endorse his claim Minos had boasted that the gods favoured him and would grant him anything he asked. To prove his boast he prepared a place for sacrifice and then called out in a very loud voice to Poseidon to send him a bull from the sea. Poseidon did indeed answer his prayer but the bull which emerged from the waves was so white and dazzlingly beautiful that Minos could not bear to kill it, and he sacrificed another in its place.

Poseidon was furious at this slight and some time later contrived to punish Minos by making his wife, Pasiphaë, fall desperately in love with the bull.

If Daedalus was taken aback when he heard Pasiphaë's somewhat unusual request that he should help her to make love with the bull, he did not show it, but instead devised an ingenious plan whereby Pasiphaë might be satisfied. Using the skill he daily displayed as he carved wooden toys, Daedalus made a life-size wooden cow. This he covered in real cow hide and placed little wheels inside carved hooves. The cow was quite hollow, and Daedalus instructed Pasiphaë to climb inside it and to open the small door in the back when the bull approached her.

Pasiphaë did as she was told and the bull mated with her. The outcome of this strange union was the hideous Minotaur, a monster with the head of a bull and the body of a man.

Minos was deeply ashamed of this horrible creature his wife

had borne and turned to Daedalus for help in hiding it. So Daedalus planned and built a Labyrinth, a building with miles and miles of winding corridors, a bewildering maze through which no one could find their way. At the very end of this he placed a room for the Minotaur.

But when Minos inevitably discovered the part that Daedalus had played in this sordid business, he ordered that Daedalus himself should be thrown into the labyrinth, and with him his son Icarus.

Pasiphaë soon heard of Daedalus's imprisonment, and as her loyalty to him was still strong, she devised a plan to set him free. But now arose a great problem, for Crete is not such a large island that it was easy for two people to hide on it indefinitely, and Daedalus knew that he would have to think of something very quickly before his absence from the Labyrinth was discovered and the people were alerted to look for him.

Daedalus planned and schemed, but there seemed no possible escape. Soon news of his freedom did reach Minos, and at once he alerted all ships, for there seemed no other way that Daedalus could escape the sea-locked island.

But in their hiding place Daedalus and Icarus were busy. With the brilliance which had marked all his former achievements Daedalus had hit upon the quite incredible idea of escaping through the air, flying as birds fly, high above the guarded ships and over the sea to safety. With amazing dexterity, and help from his beloved son, Daedalus made wings, threading the larger quill feathers together, but holding the smaller feathers together with wax.

Even as they worked the excitement of the boy grew as he ran around in circles, using his arms as wings and glowing with the anticipation of really becoming a bird for a short time.

Soon both pairs of wings were ready. As Daedalus tied Icarus's pair onto his small shoulders he told his son to stand still and listen carefully to his instructions which were quite simply that he must not fly too high, for fear of the sun's heat melting the wax and nor must he fly too low so that the high waves would splash him and wet his wings. The worried father asked the child to repeat his instructions, and hopping up and down with excitement and impatience, the child did so. Then Daedalus strapped on his own wings, and gently admonishing Icarus, he gave him a final instruction to fly always immediately behind his own path through the sky.

Again the boy promised, and somewhat reassured, Daedalus

et out, with Icarus just behind. Into the sky they both soared, he wings working exactly as Daedalus had hoped, carrying them ecurely and swiftly beyond Naxos, Delos and Paros.

Icarus was enchanted. In his wildest imaginings he had not onceived of such splendour and freedom, and soon, quite arried away with the exhilaration of the moment, and the sense f power his wings gave him, he quite forgot to follow his father's ath, and instead flew higher and higher, towards the sun.

Within minutes the increased heat had begun to melt the wax which held the little feathers together and in a panic Icarus remembered his father's warning, alas too late. Down, down the ittle figure hurtled, into the sea below and when Daedalus looked round he saw nothing in the sky behind him, but floating on the urface of the sea were some bedraggled feathers.

With a cry of grief he shouted for his son, knowing that even s he spoke all hope had gone. At once he slowed his pace and lew to where the feathers lay, and waited, mourning, until the lead body of Icarus floated up to the spot where the feathers lay.

Daedalus gathered Icarus into his arms, and carrying the child lose to him flew on to the nearest island where he buried him. The island is now called Icaria in his honour. The Icarian Sea was also named after the unfortunate child.

When Icarus was buried and Daedalus had recovered his trength, he flew on until finally he reached Sicily where he was xtremely hospitably received by the king who almost at once et him to work designing and building.

Meanwhile back in Crete Ariadne had made use of the magic all of thread she had been left by Daedalus, and by lending it to Theseus had enabled him to kill the Minotaur and evade the orrible fate set for him and his fellow Athenians. (For a full ccount see the story of Theseus.)

Minos was certainly not a man who would easily forget a wrong or an insult, and he was determined that he would find and ounish Daedalus, even if it took him the rest of his life to do so. Minos was not the inventor that Daedalus was, but he was devious nd shrewd and knew that if he could trap Daedalus then the nare most likely to succeed was Daedalus's own vanity.

With his great fleet Minos set out in search of Daedalus, and ook with him a spiraled shell which was as intricate as it was eautiful. Then he sent messengers to spread the word everywhere hat he was offering a huge reward to the person who could pass thread through this complicated shell.

Many people were excited by the challenge, but none succeeded.

Finally the Cretan fleet reached Sicily, and again the messenge
went ashore, proclaiming the reward for solving this puzzle.

Without hesitation Daedalus went to the Sicilian king, Cocalu
telling him that he could claim the prize for himself if he wou
allow Daedalus to solve the puzzle. The king agreed and sent f
the shell and when it arrived Daedalus attached a gossamer-th
thread to an ant, bored a tiny hole in the closed end of the she
through which he lured the ant by smearing honey around th
hole, then he tied the linen thread given to him by Cocalus to th
end of the gossamer thread and as the ant wandered through th
spirals it pulled with it both the threads, and Minos's puzzle wa
solved.

With pride, and glee at the thought of his great rewar
Cocalus hurried to Minos with the threaded shell. But he wa
more than a little dismayed when Minos rewarded him not wit
the prize, but with a demand to have Daedalus brought to hi
for Minos fully realised that the solution had been reached b
Daedalus, as no other man in the world was capable of solvin
so complex a problem.

Cocalus argued and shouted, swearing repeatedly that he di
not have Daedalus in his house. Again and again he swore th
this was true, but Minos refused to budge, so confident was h
that he was right. Meanwhile a messenger had slipped out an
carried the news of Minos's demands to Daedalus who was waitin
at the palace.

Finally as it was growing late, Cocalus asked Minos to con
to spend the night as his guest. Together the two went back t
the palace where Minos asked to have a bath run.

This was done, but as he lay enjoying the soothing warm wat
Cocalus's children opened a pipe above his head and through th
poured scalding water which fell down directly onto the Creta
king's head, and killed him. Next morning his body was give
back to his attendents with the explanation that he had fallen int
a pot of boiling water.

Minos was buried in Sicily, although much later his body wa
taken back to Crete. Zeus honoured him by making him one o
the three Judges of the Dead in Tartarus, along with his broth
Rhadamanthys, and his bitter enemy, Aeacus.

Daedalus lived on, continuing to build, continuing to creat
and a tradition of carving life-like dolls with moveable limb
which began with him, survives with modifications today.

*

The story of Glaucus

Glaucus was a son of Minos and Pasiphaë and much loved by both. When he was still a young child he was playing one day in the palace at Knossus, chasing a mouse, when suddenly he disappeared.

At first no one was alarmed, thinking that he was hiding to tease his family, but when evening came and he still did not appear, his parents began to grow alarmed.

For days and days Minos and Pasiphaë and all the servants searched, but to no avail. At last they turned to the Delphic Oracle for advice and were given a strangely cryptic message that the person who could give the best simile for a recent extraordinary birth on the island would find the lost boy.

News was then brought to Minos of a calf, newly-born, which changed its colour three times a day from white to red to black. Surely this was portentous! The next problem was how to interpret the news.

Finally a soothsayer, brought to Crete from Argos, pointed out the similarity of the calf to a blackberry, changing its colour just as the blackberry does when ripening.

Minos thought that this was surely the clue, and entrusted the soothsayer with the task of finding the boy.

Through the winding palace the soothsayer wandered, looking for a second omen or clue and when he noticed an owl frightening away a swarm of bees from the entrance of a room in the cellar he rushed forward, sure that this was significant.

It was. Inside the room he saw the bottom and the legs of Glaucus, whose head was buried deep into a huge jar of honey. Polyeidus, the soothsayer, took the news to Minos, satisfied that he had done all that he could, but Minos did not agree and demanded that Polyeidus restore the boy to life.

Polyeidus protested that this was quite outside his abilities, but Minos refused to listen and locked both Glaucus and Polyeidus into a tomb, saying that they would stay there until Glaucus was alive once more.

The soothsayer sat by the small corpse, almost in despair. He had with him only a sword and no idea at all as to how to cope with this seemingly insurmountable problem. Then, as his eyes grew accustomed to the dark, Polyeidus saw something moving in the tomb. He peered closer to see what it was, and then, in the darkness, saw the unmistakable shape of snake gliding towards Glaucus's body. At once he seized his sword and with one well-aimed blow, killed the snake just before it reached the boy.

Polyeidus sat back against the side of the tomb, absorbed once more in his own problems, but before long he saw yet another serpent approach the dead body of the first, hesitate and then slide back into the darkness it had emerged from. Within minutes the serpent was back again, but this time carefully balancing a herb in its mouth.

The second serpent then placed the herb on the body of the first and to Polyeidus's open-mouthed astonishment, the dead serpent moved. It had been restored to life by the herb!

At once Polyeidus acted, reaching forward and taking the herb from the back of the restored serpent and placing it on Glaucus, scarcely daring to breath as hope of escaping from this intolerable situation and certain death grew.

But the magic herb did not fail him, and within seconds Glaucus was stretching his limbs and stirring. As soon as the boy was fully awake he and Polyeidus began to shout, demanding to be freed. With cries of delight Minos had the tomb opened, praising Polyeidus extravagantly for giving him back his son.

Polyeidus was now anxious to return to his home in Argos, but Minos was not yet finished with him for he demanded that the soothsayer teach Glaucus the art of divination. Polyeidus did as he was told, but only with the greatest reluctance. However, just as he was about to board the ship to sail home he turned to Glaucus and told him to spit into his open mouth. Glaucus obeyed Polyeidus's order, spat into his mouth, and at once forgot everything he had learned.

Theseus and Ariadne

Ariadne was a daughter of Minos and Pasiphaë and a friend of Daedalus the inventor who often made her dolls when she was a child. Before he had been forced to flee from Crete Daedalus had given Ariadne a ball of thread which would enable her to find her way through the labyrinth, the winding maze which housed her half-brother, the Minotaur.

When Theseus and his party arrived from Athens, the Cretans came down to meet them and to stare at the victims. Ariadne was with them and as soon as she saw Theseus among the crowd, she fell in love with him, quite possibly prompted by Aphrodite who also favoured Theseus.

With courage and determination Ariadne stole out under cover of night to where the Athenians were lodged and having found Theseus she gave him the magic ball of thread, telling him that with this he could find his way through the laybrinth to kill the Minotaur, and find his way out again to safety; but that when he left the island he must take her with him as she knew that she loved him.

Theseus readily agreed, for he longed to kill the Minotaur and save his companions; and to marry the beautiful Ariadne seemed no hardship either.

Ariadne gave him his instructions very clearly. Theseus was to open the entrance door, tie the hanging end of the thread to the stone over the doorway to secure it and the ball would then roll along, finding its own way to the depths of the labyrinth where the Minotaur lived. The man-bull should then be killed, sacrificed to Poseidon, and by following the thread as he wound it again, Theseus would find his way out of the maze.

Everything went just as Ariadne had planned. Theseus killed the Minotaur with a sword given to him by Ariadne and without any difficulty found his way back to his waiting companions. The seven youths had overcome their guards and found their way out, and the girls had been saved by the two among their party who were really effeminate looking but fearless boys. The Athenians embraced each other with delight, scarcely able to believe their lucky escape. They then raced to the harbour where their ship was waiting to carry them to safety. After a brief battle at the harbour, with no Athenian lives lost, the party began to row as fast as they were able, putting Crete far behind them.

Ariadne was very happy. Sitting beside her beloved Theseus and revelling in the shared joy of the Athenians she scarcely had a thought for the reaction of her parents when they found her gone.

After some days of rowing, the ship landed at Naxos, which was then named Dia. The young people all leapt overboard, delighted to be on land for some hours.

Ariadne decided to take a nap, enjoying stretching out to the full, for the boat in which they were travelling was small and cramped.

Theseus now did an extraordinary thing. Seeing that Ariadne was fast asleep, he quickly gathered together his companions, and they sailed away, leaving the girl alone on the island.

There are several explanations for this, though none very reasonable. Some say that a few days of her company had wearied Theseus and that his eye had been saught by one of the Athenians. Perhaps he was afraid of the effect that Ariadne's presence would have on the people of Athens, or perhaps he too had slept, and dreamt that Dionysus was warning him against taking Ariadne off, for the god of the vine (also frequently known by his Roman name of Bacchus) wanted Ariadne himself.

But whatever his reason, Theseus, the hero of Athens left the girl without a word; no thanks for her help and no goodbye.

Note: Theseus's story is vividly recreated in two fascinating novels by Mary Renault. These are *The Bull From The Sea* and *The King Must Die*. (New English Library Paperbacks.)

NAXOS

Ariadne and Dionysus

When Ariadne woke up from her sleep and found that Theseus had left her she was in despair. Scarcely believing her misfortune she ran from one end of the island to the other, hoping that he was gone only from sight.

But finally she realised that he really had deserted her and weak, frightened and hurt she fell to the ground weeping.

It was not long, however, before she was interrupted by Dionysus, who appeared in front of her with a group of Satyrs and Maenads.

Dionysus was god of the vine, a son of Zeus and the mortal Semele, herself a daughter of King Cadmus of Thebes. He was the only one of the gods whose parents were not both divine.

Dionysus had a strange start in life for when his mother was carrying him, Zeus told Semele that she could have anything at all that she wished. He loved her passionately and longed to please her, but when she told him that what she really wanted was to see him in all his splendour as King of Heaven Zeus was shocked for he knew that no mortal could stand the sight, and that she would see him and die. This was in fact Hera's plan, for jealous once again, she had planted in Semele's mind the notion to make this particular request.

Zeus sadly agreed, for he could not break his promise. And when Semele tried to look on the burning lightning and thunder that was Zeus, she did indeed die instantly, but Hermes seized the child from her womb and sewed it up inside Zeus's thigh until the baby had reached full-term, and was born again. This explains his name, which means 'twice-born'.

Even when born, Dionysus's troubles were far from over. Hera had him torn to shreds and boiled, but Rhea (his grandmother) brought him to life again. Zeus then had him disguised as a girl so that Hera would not notice him, but she was not deceived and

drove the couple who were caring for him to their deaths
Dionysus was then transformed into a goat, and lovingly cared
for by some nymphs who fed him on honey. It was during the
time that he lived with the nymphs on Mount Nysa that
Dionysus invented wine, for which he has been celebrated ever
since.

As a man he was somewhat effeminate (as a result of his troubled
early life) and Hera made him temporarily mad. He wandered all
over the known world, accompanied by his tutor Silenus and the
Satyrs and Maenads. His travels took him to Egypt, India and
Europe, and wherever he went he taught the art of vinegrowing
and wine-making; but additionally Dionysus had certain military
successes and founded some cities.

He was always associated with both joy and terror, just as wine
is. The Satyrs who accompanied Dionysus were, like Pan, half
man and half goat. (The goat was a symbol of virility.) They were
the spirits of the wild life of the hills and woods. Satyrs are always
described as very lusty creatures, constantly in a state of sexual
excitement. Their lives were devoted to amusement, especially
dancing and their arrival was always preceded by the clashing
of their cymbals. Generally cowardly they could occasionally be
belligerent and aggressive when drunk. The trunk and head of a
satyr would be rather like that of a man, but the head was capped
with little horns, pricked ears and below the waist they had legs of
a goat.

> She was foaming at the mouth,
> and her crazed eyes
> rolled with frenzy. She was mad, quite mad,
> possessed by Bacchus.

This description of a Maenad shows these women (said to have
come from Asia) at their most extreme, ready to tear apart a living
creature, as they did to Orpheus, in the frenzy of a Bacchanalian
revelry. These strange women were thought to be unnaturally
strong, able to tear men, bulls or goats to pieces with their bare
hands. But they had a strange affinity with animals too, and in a
gentle mood fed kids and fawns from their breasts. They were
immune from burning by fire and could (so it was said) produce
strange miracles such as making fountains of milk or wine spring
from the ground.

Both Satyrs and Meanads searched, through these excesses, to
become part of the god himself whom they saw as the god of
fertility.

When Dionysus and his followers found Ariadne she was weeping and despairing and refused at first to be distracted. But Dionysus was a determined adversary of misery and forced her to listen to his promise of love, saying that he would take care of her always, unlike the faithless Theseus.

Ariadne tried three times to run from the god, to be alone with her misery, but he refused to let her go, telling her that he would never leave her as the faithless Theseus had done but would marry her then and there. So finally she agreed, at once forgetting Theseus and his unkindness.

Dionysus was a delighted bridegroom and told Ariadne that her wedding gift would be the sky itself, and taking her crown from her head he transformed the jewels into shining stars and set it in heaven as the constellation *Corona Borealis*.

Ariadne quickly became the most devoted of wives and joined Dionysus in his journeying through the world, establishing his practices and worship.

Finally, when it was clear that men needed little further encouragement in their worship of the vine, Dionysus went to live in Olympus. Zeus wished to honour him by making him one of the Twelve, but there was no place for him until sweet, bashful Hestia offered to resign her place to make room for the god of the vine. The goddess was in fact only too delighted to have such an ideal excuse to leave the great table, for the endless intrigues and squabbling of the gods and goddesses had worn her down.

Dionysus was given permission to honour his mother whom he brought up from Tartarus, having first successfully bribed Persephone (despite Hera's objection to this favouring of an old rival). Zeus himself gave Semele quarters in Olympus, although her name was changed to avoid causing friction and jealousy among those ghosts still left in Tartarus.

> And as I sat, over the light blue hills
> There came a noise of revellers: the rills
> Into the wide stream came of purple hue –
>   'Twas Bacchus and his crew!
> The earnest trumpet spake, and silver thrills
> From kissing cymbals made a merry din –
>   'Twas Bacchus and his kin!
> Like to a moving vintage down they came,
> Crown'd with green leaves, and faces all on flame;
> All madly dancing through the pleasant valley.
>
>   Keats

DELOS

The Birth of Artemis and Apollo

Leto, mother of Apollo and Artemis, was a daughter of the Titans Phoebe and Coeus, and herself goddess of night. She was much loved by Zeus, which did her little good as she now invoked Hera's jealousy and wrath, and when the time came near for Leto to give birth she found that Hera had sent Iris and Ares to travel the land, warning the people against giving Leto shelter or hospitality, and had decreed that Leto would not give birth in any place where the sun shone.

So Leto wandered desperately through Attica, Thrace, Euboea and the islands of the Aegean, rejected everywhere that she went, and constantly tormented by the serpent Python, the Dragon of Delphi, which Hera had sent to increase her troubles.

When tired almost beyond endurance Leto found her way to a small pool and paused to drink and refresh herself, but some passers-by, inspired by Hera, roughly told her to get up and move on. Then, when they saw that she did not, they pushed Leto aside and jumped into the water, stirring it up with their feet and making it muddy and undrinkable.

In desperation Leto called out to Zeus who had so cruelly left her to her troubles, and Zeus at once changed the men into frogs, who have, since this time, always been found near muddy pools.

At last, carried in the gentle arms of the wind (or, some say, on the back of a dolphin) Leto came to Ortygia, the Island of Quails, a tiny islet barely separate from Delos, itself a rocky floating island. On Ortygia Leto gave birth to Artemis, and then helped by her newly-born daughter she crossed to Delos.

Delos too tried to refuse her, saying that as it was such an ugly rocky island Apollo would, when born, despise it and push it under the sea. But Leto promised the island that on the contrary, Apollo would be so grateful to the island that he would honour it by building on it a great temple.

So Delos gave Leto refuge and because it had been prophesied that Apollo would be born in a place where the sun did not shine, Poseidon sent a huge wave over the island, like a great net, which kept out the light of the sun for the nine days and nights that Leto was again in labour.

Finally, between an olive tree and a date palm, Leto gave birth to Apollo, 'the most Greek of all the gods'.

Poseidon then anchored Delos to one spot with four pillars which rose up beneath the island.

The islands which encircle and protect Delos are called the Cyclades, and Delos became one of the greatest, at one time the political and religious centre of the Aegean.

The very earliest Greeks forbade (as far as possible) either birth or death to take place on Apollo's island and in 426 BC this was again decreed and the pregnant and dying were taken to nearby Rhenia, perhaps the original 'Quails Island'.

A vast precinct, the Hieron of Apollo, still stands in part on Delos, its temples, altars and statues giving the visitor at least an impression of the place that Apollo held in Greek hearts during a thousand years of worship.

The sea god Glaucus

It is always somewhat confusing when two figures emerge from Greek mythology with the same name, but the Glaucus of Delos is not to be confused with Glaucus, son of Minos, whose story is told elsewhere in this book.

Glaucus of this story was originally a humble fisherman from Aethedonia. One evening as he returned home in the last of the light from a day's fishing he placed his dead fish on some grass which, though Glaucus didn't know it, had been planted by Cronus (father of Zeus) during the wonderful Golden Age.

The grass had miraculous restorative properties and the fish at once leapt back to life and threw themselves into the water. Glaucus was mystified, but picked a little of the grass and put it into his own mouth. At once he was transformed into a Triton (an immortal merman) and so he joined his fish and went to live in the sea too where he was welcomed by the other divinities and proclaimed a marine god.

Glaucus is well known for his love-affairs – all of which were unsuccessful. When Theseus left Ariadne alone on Naxos he rushed to console her, but as soon as Dionysus arrived the god of the vine bound poor Glaucus with vine-shoots and threw him back into the sea.

This sea god's home was an underwater palace off the coast of Delos and he would leave it once a year to visit all the islands and ports of Greece to give the sailors predictions, usually of a sinister nature.

EUBOEA

Poseidon, God of Earthquakes and of the Sea

After the brothers, Zeus, Hades and Poseidon had deposed their father Cronus, they drew lots from a helmet as to which part of the universe each should rule.

To Zeus went the sky, the greatest prize of all; to Hades went the Underworld and to Poseidon the sea. This made Poseidon equal to his brothers in dignity, but not in power and because of this he was frequently disgruntled and disagreeable.

Poseidon built himself a splendid underwater palace off Aegae in the Euboean Gulf. His wife was Amphitrite, who may have been a Nereid, though some call her the mother of the Nereids; others say that she was the daughter of Oceanus and the female personification of the sea.

It would appear that Amphitrite was an unwilling bride for when Poseidon began to pay attention to her she fled from the island of Naxos where she had been playing to hide with Atlas, but a dolphin sent in pursuit by Poseidon eventually found her and carried her back to the sea-god who was so grateful that he turned the dolphin into a constellation.

> Along the deep
> With beauteous ankles, Amphitrite glides
> Hesiod (Elton's tr.)

Like Hera, Zeus's reluctant bride, Amphitrite once married became a jealous and possessive wife, and like Hera, she had a great many opportunities to exercise her jealousy for Poseidon had love affairs with goddesses, nymphs and mortals, but Amphitrite, unlike Hera, rarely took spiteful revenge on the object of her husband's love.

In his passion for Demeter, the corn-goddess, Poseidon shows the same lack of sensitivity for her feelings that Zeus so frequently showed to his 'loved ones'. When Demeter had lost her daughter Persephone to Hades, god of the underworld and Poseidon's brother, Demeter wandered sadly through the land searching for her. Poseidon was touched by her sadness and conceived a great passion for her. But Demeter was not in the mood for Poseidon or anyone else, and so she changed herself into a mare, thinking that in this way she could avoid him. In her new shape she stood among a herd, but despite her efforts Poseidon found her out and transformed himself into a stallion so that she could not escape him. This unhappy union resulted in the conception of the wild horse Arion who was gifted with the power of speech. Demeter never forgave Poseidon and her anger was such that she was sometimes known as 'Demeter the Fury'.

With Medusa* too Poseidon conceived a horse, the magic winged horse Pegasus, which sprang from Medusa's dead body after she had been decapitated by Perseus.

With Astypalaea, a sister of Europa, Poseidon had two children, Ancaeus the Argonaut and Eurypylus who was to rule the island of Cos in the Sporades.

One rather curious story about Poseidon's love is that of Mestra, the daughter of King Erysichthon of Thessaly. He was one of the very few sufferers at the hand of Demeter for generally she was one of the kindest and most gentle of goddesses, but Erysichthon invaded a grove which had been dedicated to her and began to cut down her trees to make a banqueting hall for himself. Demeter adopted human form and asked Erysichthon to stop, but the king refused to do so and threatened Demeter with his axe. The goddess then resumed her own shape and told a horrified Erysichthon that he was condemned to be always insatiably hungry.

Erysichthon returned home and began to eat, but no matter how much or for how long he ate, nothing could appease his terrible, gnawing hunger. His family and friends helped him as much as they could, but soon he was reduced to begging and eating filth from the road. Finally he decided to sell Mestra to gain a little more money to buy food, but Poseidon was so much in love with her that he gave her a cunning way both to protect herself and to keep her father in constant funds. She would stand on the beach until someone approached; a transaction would take place and then when her new owner had turned his back Mestra would quickly metamorphose herself into a small creature so that the

* (see the story of Perseus).

uyer could not find her, and would see only a tiny insect crawling way along a beach.

The same pattern occurred many times, to the satisfaction of ll, but finally news spread of Erysichthon's trick and buyers no nger arrived. Starving and desperate, Erysichthon had no lternative but to eat himself.

Amphitrite showed her jealous face most obviously in the story f Scylla, a daughter of Phorcys, who was bathing in her pool one ay when Amphitrite threw into the water some magical herbs hich immediately changed Scylla into a barking monster with velve feet and six heads. Scylla became a menace to all sailors, or those unlucky enough to pass her cave (traditionally located the Straits of Messina) would be seized by the now monstrous rl, and eaten.

oseidon is sometimes credited with having given men the first orse, and certainly horses are frequently associated with him. In is underwater palace he kept a stable of white chariot horses ith hooves of bronze and manes of gold. They pulled his golden nariot which he would drive over the waves calming them, no natter how fierce the storm.

In his hand Poseidon usually carried his trident – a three-ronged spear, given to him by the Cyclopes during the war gainst Cronus, with which he could shatter whatever he pleased. s earthquake god he is credited with some good, namely creat-g the pass of Peneios, a natural drain which carries water from ne plain of Thessaly.

Poseidon's skill with his trident is given as the means by which ne islands were created for, as the story goes, during the war ith the Giants when the Olympians were fighting to win control, oseidon split whole mountainsides with his trident, and these lled into the sea to become islands.

Despite his power over the sea, the lakes and the river, Poseidon as constantly jealous of Zeus and once plotted with Hera and ne other gods to dethrone him. The plot, however, failed, and as s punishment Poseidon was ordered to spend a year at Troy ong with Apollo in the service of Laomedon, the king (perhaps son of Heracles).

During this year Poseidon built the great walls of Troy helped y Aeacus (whose story is also recounted in this book), while pollo played his lyre and watched Laomedon's flocks. But at ne end of this year Laomedon refused to honour the payment he had promised the three for their work, and Apollo and Poseidon were very angry and during the great Trojan war energetically helped the Greeks against the Trojans.

To punish Laomedon Poseidon sent a great sea monster to Laomedon's land which destroyed the crops by spewing sea water all over them. In despair Laomedon turned to an oracle for advice and was told that he must expose his daughter Hesione on a rock in the sea and allow the monster to devour her.

Laomedon was horrified, and tried to persuade some of the other nobles to sacrifice their daughters instead. But all refused, saying that the fault lay with Laomedon and he alone must pay the price.

So Hesione was chained to a rock on the Trojan shore, quite naked except for her jewels. While she was shivering there, waiting for death, Heracles and Telamon (a son of Aeacus) happened to pass by. Heracles at once released her and carried her to the city, where he told her father that he would destroy the monster if Laomedon would give him in exchange the two immortal horses which could run over land or sea given to Laomedon by Zeus when the god had fallen in love with Ganymedes, Laomedon's son.

Laomedon was so delighted that his daughter was to be saved from a fearful death that he agreed at once, and Heracles set out to kill the monster.

As he approached it, the great creature opened its mouth wide and Heracles leapt inside it. There he stayed for three days fighting the monster from within, until finally it died and Heracles crawled out victorious, though without his hair.

But once more Laomedon proved himself to be a dishonourable man for he tried to pass by his promise to Heracles by giving him ordinary horses. Heracles was so angry that he made war on Troy, killing Laomedon and all his sons except Priam whom he proclaimed king.

(Note: There were ten Troys in all and this was not *the* Trojan War which occurred some years later when Priam's son Paris abducted Helen and took her to the now rebuilt Troy and the Greeks followed in pursuit to rescue her, resulting in a war which lasted for ten years and left Troy, Asia's proudest city, in smouldering ruins.)

The children that Poseidon and Amphitrite had together were not particularly distinguished though they included Rhode, after whom Rhodes is named; some nameless sons who attacked

Aphrodite during her voyage from Cythera to Cyprus, and Triton,
a merman who is human from the waist up and fish-shaped below.

> King of the stormy sea!
> Brother of Jove and co-inheritor
> Of elements! Eternally before
> Thee the waves awful bow. Fast, stubborn rock,
> At thy fear'd trident shrinking, doth unlock
> Its deep foundations, hissing into foam.
> All mountain-rivers, lost in the wide home
> Of thy capacious bosom, ever flow.
>
> O shell-borne king sublime!
> We lay our hearts before thee evermore –
> We sing, and we adore.
>
> 　　　　　　　　Keats

AEGINA

The naming of Aegina and the birth of Aeacus

Zeus's lust is well known, and stories of his passions spring u
constantly throughout Greek mythology. But always, as in th
story of his love for Aegina, Zeus's passion must be followed by
story of Hera's revenge.

Aegina's father was the River-god Asopus, her mother, Metop
a daughter of the river Ladon. Together Aegina's parents ha
only two sons, but many daughters, some say twenty. The girls
the family were very beautiful and in turn Zeus, Apollo a
Poseidon had paid them overt attention.

Aegina was one of twins and her twin sister Thebe (after who
Thebes is named) had been one of Zeus's early victims. Wh
Aegina too disappeared it did not take Asopus very long to co
clude why she had gone, and anxiously he went in pursuit of h
daughter.

At last he found the errant pair in a wood, where Zeus w
kissing Aegina and embracing her. Zeus was angry and emba
rassed at being discovered and at once fled, running through t
trees until he was out of sight, and then changing himself into
rock until his newest love and her father had disappeared in t
direction of their home. But once they had gone he lost no time
all in hurrying straight back to Olympus and seizing his thunde
bolts, rained them down upon the hapless River-god who w
never again able to move with his former agility and speed.

Zeus's ardour was unabated, and as single-minded as ever,
went again to Aegina and took her off to an island where th
could continue to be together. Now it was in the shape of an ea
that he laid with her, and soon she had a son, who was nam
Aeacus.

News of Zeus's adventures never escaped Hera, and when s
had heard of the birth of a son to Zeus, she at once resolved
punish the girl, who had in fact done nothing to deserve

goddess's virulent anger. But Hera was never reasonable, and decided to punish not only Aegina but to include all the inhabitants of the island in her punishment as well.

Aeacus was by now a young man, and to honour his mother he had changed the name of the island from its original Oenone to Aegina, in her honour. He was king of Aegina, and Hera resolved to deprive him of all his subjects by slipping a serpent into a stream on the island. The serpent then laid thousands of eggs which hatched unnaturally quickly and squirmed out of the water to wriggle over the fields, spreading over the whole island and into every river and stream. A plague fell on the people; no rain fell and a strange heat and darkness hovered over the island and to make matters worse a strong wind blew from the south for four months.

Neither crops, nor buildings, nor people could survive. The wretched islanders died a horrible death as wracked with thirst they drank the foul waters of the rivers, poisoned by the ever-increasing serpents.

Aeacus watched his people and his hopes dying, and was powerless to help. His prayers to Zeus seemed to have gone unanswered, and nothing could now save his island.

Then one night in desperation Aeacus called out loudly to Zeus, begging and pleading with his father to help him to make the land beautiful again, to fill it with men and with fine crops, and to rid Aegina of the hideous destructive serpents. Inspired by the sight of the tiny industrious ants carrying some last grains of corn up a nearby tree, he implored Zeus to give him as many men as there were ants on the oak.

The oak tree was sacred to Zeus, and shook as Aeacus spoke. But Aeacus was no longer frightened, for all other hope had gone, and so he fell to his knees and kissed the oak repeatedly, calling again and again to Zeus for help.

During that night Aeacus had a strange and very vivid dream, that all the ants he had seen that day really had been transformed into men. When he woke the dream was still as real, but he dismissed it from his mind as nonsense until suddenly his son Telamon came running to him shouting that there were strong fine men walking across the fields. When Aeacus went outside he saw that his son's words were true, that rain had begun to fall and the serpents had disappeared.

These men, sprung from ants, were called Myrmidons, and they and their many descendants displayed all the characteristics so admired in ants – tenacity, patience and industry.

With the Myrmidons' help, Aegina became great again, and Aeacus was noted for his devotion to Zeus and his piety. To protect the island from invading pirates he made it something of a fortress, but despite the difficulties of reaching him, men would come from the mainland to ask for his advice and intercession with the gods.

Aeacus played a part in building the walls of Troy, when Apollo and Poseidon needed the help of a mortal to ensure the strength of the walls; though the walls of Troy were not to remain invincible and two of Aeacus's sons, Telamon and Ajax, were to take part in the great Trojan War.

When he died Aeacus was appointed one of the three Judges of the Dead, along with two other sons of Zeus, Minos and Rhadamanthys

> . . . as my bark did skim
> The bright blue waters with a fanning wind,
> Came Megara before me, and behind
> Aegina lay, Piraeus on the right,
> And Corinth on the left; I lay reclined
> Along the prow, and saw all these unite
> In ruin, as he had seen the desolate sight.
>
> Byron

Aphaea, goddess of Aegina

Visitors to Aegina will undoubtedly include in their itinerary a trip to the Temple of Aphaela, built at the end of the 6th Century BC, or the early years of the 5th Century BC on the site of two earlier temples. In the 1950's it was partly re-erected and is now certainly the most splendid temple to be found on the islands, and is rivalled on the mainland only by the Theseum in Athens and the temple of Bassae in the Peloponnese. To see this temple alone, a visit to Aegina would be justified.

Despite his marriage to Pasiphaë, Minos of Crete was constantly pursuing other women, and one of those he chased with the greatest persistence was a girl called Britomartis, or sometimes, as on Aegina, called Aphaea.

Aphaea was the daughter of Leto, who was also mother to Apollo and Artemis and certainly whether or not she was Artemis's sister, the goddess of hunting took great care of Aphaea, entrusting her with the care of her hounds, and taking her hunting with her.

Aphaea is credited with the invention of hunting-nets.

The attentions of Minos were most unwelcomed by her, and she tried frantically to avoid him. But he chased her relentlessly for nine months until she could bear it no longer and thinking that death was preferable to such a miserable life, she threw herself into the sea, but instead of drowning was rescued by some kindly fishermen. Artemis had her deified, and the people of Aegina called her by the name of Aphaea because this means vanisher, which is precisely what she did.

CYTHERA

Aphrodite, Goddess of Desire

Uranus (Heaven) fathered the Titans, who were supreme before the Olympians, on Mother Earth. When Uranus was displaced by his son Cronus, the leader of the Titans, Cronus castrated him and held up his bleeding genitals, so that the blood dripped down onto the earth below. From this blood Mother Earth bore the Three Furies, and the Nymphs of the ash-tree.

The genitals themselves were cast off into the sea, fertilising the foam which collected on them, and from this foam was born Aphrodite who sprang from it fully grown and rode on a scallop shell to the island of Cythera.

> Look, look why shine
> Those floating bubbles with such light divine?
> They break, and from their mist a lily form
> Rises from out the wave, in beauty warm.
> The wave is by the blue-veined feet scare press'd,
> Her silky ringlets float about her breast,
> Veiling its fairy loveliness; while her eye
> Is soft and deep as the blue heaven is high.
> The Beautiful is born; and sea and earth
> May well revere the hour of the mysterious birth.
>
> Shelley

Aphrodite did not stay long at Cythera however, but instead crossed the sea to Cyprus. Both islands are sacred to her, and associated with her.

> The breath of the west wind bore her
> Over the sounding sea,
> Up from the delicate foam,
> To wave-ringed Cyprus, her isle.
>
> Homer

The Goddess of desire is always associated with beauty and tenderness and she only very occasionally uses her power maliciously towards men.

The Fates assigned to her one duty, and one only; namely to make love, but on one occasion she was discovered by Athene weaving quietly on a loom. At once Athene complained, and Aphrodite apologised to the goddess of weaving for usurping her tasks, and never again tried to extend the scope of her duties.

Aphrodite was nothing if not generous and had many many lovers, both mortal and divine. She was the owner of a marvellous girdle which she guarded jealously and when she was wearing this, no one could resist her. Strangely enough, considering their general separate wantonness, Zeus and Aphrodite never made love, though when she wore her girdle, he was often tempted. Rather spitefully Zeus once made her fall in love, and to humiliate her further chose as Aphrodite's loved one a mere mortal.

The young man, who was named Anchises, a son of the King of the Dardanians, was extremely handsome and many women had been in love with him but he was nevertheless quite dazzled when Aphrodite appeared at his bedside, despite the fact that she had disguised herself as a mere princess. The bed was covered with luxurious skins, and Aphrodite lay down on the skins beside her lover and together they spent a blissful night.

In the morning Aphrodite revealed to Anchises who she really was. Poor Anchises was quite horrified for he was afraid that he would now have to die, having been intimate with a goddess. But Aphrodite reassured him, telling him that all would be well so long as he didn't tell anyone of their night together. This Anchises willingly promised.

However, some day slater Anchises was drinking wine with some friends, and one of them asked him if he would prefer to spend the night with a particular high-born girl, or Aphrodite herself. The wine had weakened Anchises' caution and barely noticing his words he replied that as he had already made love to both the question did not apply.

Zeus himself heard these words, and was very angry, though considering his part in the affair this scarcely seems justified. Right or wrong notwithstanding, he hurled a thunderbolt at Anchises which would have killed him, but Aphrodite was watching her lover too and threw her girdle between the man and the thunderbolt so that it landed at his feet. But the shock itself was so great that Anchises was transfixed in a bent position, never again able to straighten up, and Aphrodite soon lost interest in him.

From this union however was born a son named Aeneas (subject of *The Aeneid*, greatest of all Latin poems) who was one of the most famous heroes of the Trojan War, fighting on the Trojan side.

Aphrodite had a much longer-lasting affair with Ares, the god of war. He was very much disliked by all the other Olympians but Aphrodite found him exciting and together they had several children, Phobus, Deimus and Harmonia, whom Aphrodite passed off as the children of her husband, Hephaestus.

It seems again spiteful of Zeus to have married the goddess of love and desire to the ugliest of all the gods, and certainly it does not seem to have been to much purpose, for Aphrodite was constantly leaving Hephaestus to find amusement elsewhere.

Hephaestus was usually very kind to her, and because he loved her so desperately, he was generally forgiving.

Aphrodite loved Hermes, Zeus's lively winged messenger, too, and from their union Hermaphroditus was born. This was a dual sexed creature built like a youth but with finely formed breasts and long hair.

Eros was generally thought to be another of Aphrodite's sons, though some say that without Eros (whose name means sexual passion) no one else could have been born and that he himself was hatched from the world-egg at the same time as Mother Earth and Tartarus (the Underworld) were born.

The father of Eros (if he was indeed Aphrodite's son) could have been either Hermes or Ares.

Although he was never important enough to take his place among the ruling twelve Olympians, Eros's role in the world has always been an important one. He was a wild and lovely youth, who regarded his power to set hearts aflame with love as something of a joke, and was generally totally careless and indiscriminate about where he aimed his little golden arrows.

Despite her many lovers Aphrodite renewed her virginity regularly in the sea near Paphos.

POROS

The naming of Cape Skylli

Minos of Crete was acknowledged by all to be a very great king indeed. He ruled over many cities in Crete and extended his power outside the island too, clearing the Mediterranean of pirates and claiming control over the sea. He was not a man to be easily thwarted, and was ruthless when crossed.

When news was brought to Minos that his son Androgeus had been killed during a stay in Athens his reaction was immediate. Gathering his army around him Minos went calling on the kings of the neighbouring islands to ask for their help to take revenge against the Athenians.

Some of the kings readily gave him their support, for whatever they felt in their hearts they were afraid to offend him. Others were more courageous, but if like Aeacus of Aegina they dared to refuse Minos, they quickly joined the ranks of his sworn enemies. The enmity between Aeacus and Minos continued even after death, for both were appointed Judges of the Dead along with Rhadamanthys, Minos's brother and through their father Zeus, half-brothers to Aeacus. But brothers or not, Minos and Aeacus remained in bitter opposition.

Athens had an extremely strong and faithful ally in the city of Nisa on the Isthmus of Corinth. The name of the city was later changed to Megara (as it is called today). This city was ruled by Nisus the Egyptian who was a firm friend and supporter of Aegeus of Athens, so Minos decided that he would lay seige to the city and set out with his armies, sure of an early victory.

But the seige proved to be a drawn-out affair, neither side gaining nor losing much.

Inside the city was a high tower, said to have been built by Poseidon and Apollo. While they were building it Apollo had rested his lyre against a pile of stones at the base of the tower, and since that time a pebble dropped on the stones would ping with the sound of a string being pulled on a lyre.

King Nisus's daughter Scylla never tired of dropping pebbles down from the top of this tower, and loved hearing the music as they hit the stones below. She always spent part of her day in the tower playing this game.

During the siege of her father's city Scylla continued to go to the tower, but now passed at least half of her time there staring at the soldiers of both sides, for from the vantage point of the tower she could see everything that happened beneath her.

Soon soldier-spotting became even more enjoyable than music-making and after weeks of watching Scylla was well enough informed to know who was who and what their duties were.

All the soldiers on both sides were very brave, but the figure that Scylla watched most constantly and with the greatest admiration was that of Minos. He was everywhere; running and plotting and supervising and ordering. The girl was quite fascinated and as she stared at him day after day she fell quite obsessively in love with this man, her father's enemy.

The girl quickly learned that the siege was not going particularly well for either side, for as she listened to her father's grave conversations she realised that there was something of an impasse, which neither side could seem to overcome.

Scylla knew, as all his subjects did, that her father had a claim to immortality through a purple lock of hair which grew from the centre of his head. As long as he had this lock, no one could kill him. This knowledge gave the people of Nisa great courage, for their strategy depended on the king's wisdom and experience but they believed that no matter what risks the king took, he was inviolable.*

Days passed and Scylla's obsession with Minos grew, and all other loyalties faded as she considered how best to win him. Suddenly she knew what the answer was! She would present him with her father's lock of purple hair and when he had overcome Nisa he would be so grateful that he would make her his wife.

Scylla was delighted with this plan and that very night went into her father's room, cut off the precious lock of hair, stole the keys to the city gates and under the cover of darkness, reached Minos's tent which she had long since landmarked.

* Readers of *Land of Zeus* will remember a very similar story about Pterelaus whose immortality depended on a single lock of golden hair which was pulled from him by his daughter Comaitho in an attempt to win the love of Amphitryon.

When King Minos saw what the girl carried he could scarcely believe his good fortune. It was his, said Scylla, in exchange for offering his love to her. Minos agreed and spent the night with his new accomplice, then as dawn broke he and his armies stormed the opened city gates and took the city of Nisa.

But as soon as he had won the city Minos turned on Scylla and told her that as she had betrayed her father he would have nothing more to do with her. The girl was aghast, for she genuinely believed that she had committed patricide in the greatest of all causes, her love for Minos.

Scylla begged and pleaded, but Minos cast her aside and prepared his men to leave again for Crete.

As the ships moved out of the harbour Scylla threw herself into the sea to swim after Minos, still unable to believe that he was rejecting her. Desperately she clung to the stern of the ship, her face awash with tears and salt foam. Then suddenly her father's soul in the shape of an eagle came down and viciously pecked her. Too frightened and exhausted to cling any longer, Scylla fell back into the sea and drowned. Her soul too was turned into a bird, an owl which was constantly pursued by an angry eagle.

The headland of Poros, now known as Cape Skylli, was renamed in memory of Scylla, the sad and foolish girl.

Minos returned to Crete and called on Zeus, his father, to avenge the Athenians for Androgeus's death and this Zeus did by sending earthquakes which continued until the Athenians were forced to go to Minos to ask him what atonement he would accept. Then Minos made the cruel demand that the Athenians should send seven youths and seven maidens every Great Year (every nine years) to be captured in the labyrinth by the Minotaur, the hideous creature, half-man and half-bull which had been born to Minos's wife Pasiphaë. (This story is told in the chapter on Daedalus, the architect who designed the labyrinth.)

Two parties of young Athenians were devoured by the Minotaur before Theseus himself went to Crete with the third, and with the help of Ariadne, Minos's daughter, slew the Minotaur and ended the terrible punishment.

SERIPHOS

Danaë and her son Perseus

Danaë was one of the most beautiful girls who ever lived, and much loved by her father Acrisius, the King of Argos. The king had no sons, and pinned all his hopes for an heir on his lovely daughter. But one day an oracle predicted that Acrisius would die at the hand of Danaë's son, so to ensure that this could not happen, Acrisius locked Danaë up at the top of a high bronze tower which was guarded day and night.

The girl was not exactly unhappy there, but she was very lonely and when Zeus noticed this he decided to take advantage of the situation, especially as Danaë was the sort of beauty he most admired.

So Zeus came to Danaë in a shower of gold and lay with her, and from this meeting Danaë became pregnant and eventually gave birth to a son, whom she named Perseus.

When Acrisius heard that Danaë had a child which she claimed to be Zeus's, he refused to believe her, thinking instead that his own brother, who was an enemy of old, had somehow escaped the guard and reached the girl, making her pregnant himself.

Acrisius considered the idea of killing Danaë and her child, but his love for his daughter would not allow him to do so, and instead he put them both into a huge chest which he pushed out to sea, leaving it to fate to decide whether they should live or die.

Inside the chest Danaë held her tiny child close to her and hoped and prayed that when daylight broke they would find themselves washed up on a friendly beach.

The chest was actually rocking over the waves towards Seriphos, perhaps guided by Zeus, for there on the beach at Seriphos was a fisherman who noticed the strange object bobbing on the sea, and dragged it to shore. When he opened the chest and saw a woman and baby inside he was most surprised, but collected his wits about him and took them to the home of his brother Polydectes who was king of the island.

Polydectes took them in and brought up Perseus like a son. All would have been well but Polydectes also wished to regard Danaë as one of the family and to make her his wife; and this she would not allow. Polydectes knew that Perseus supported Danaë's refusal of him and decided that she would weaken if her son was removed from his position of influence.

For some time Polydectes considered the possibilities open to him and then with great cunning he announced that he wished to compete for the hand of Hippodameia (see *The Naming Of The Myrtoan Sea*), but needed horses to offer as a bridal gift.

Just as Polydectes expected, Perseus was delighted to hear that the king had lost interest in Danaë, and he at once went to Polydectes saying that while he could not help with the horses Polydectes had only to name another gift and Perseus would do what he could to ensure that Polydectes would have it.

Polydectes then looked straight at the trustful Perseus, thanked him for his offer, and asked him to bring back the head of the Gorgon Medusa. This, Polydectes said, was the only gift he wanted.

The Gorgons were some of the many hideous children of Phorcys and his sister Ceto, divinities of the sea. They had originally been beautiful but when Medusa, one of the Gorgons, was in love with Poseidon she had been sufficiently indiscreet to allow him to make love to her in a temple sacred to Athene. To punish her Athene changed all three sisters into winged monsters with bulbous eyes, revoltingly long teeth, a protruding tongue, bronze claws where fingers should have been, and snakes instead of hair. Merely to look upon one of these creatures would turn a man to stone.

Perseus grew pale with alarm, but Athene had overheard the conversation and hating Medusa still she combined forces with Hermes to help Perseus overcome her old enemy.

Because he must at all costs avoid looking Medusa in the face and thus being petrified, Athene gave to Perseus a brightly polished bronze shield in which he could see a reflection of the Gorgon, and Hermes presented him with a sword which was so strong it would not bend when it hit the scales on Medusa's neck. The gods then sent him to see the Graea, sisters of the Gorgons who had only one eye and one tooth between them which they passed from sister to sister. These strange swan-shaped women lived in a dark land which saw light neither from the sun nor from the moon. Hermes himself guided Perseus to them and then watched as Perseus cunningly and quickly intercepted the eye as one Graea passed it to the next. For a moment each sister thought that one of the other two must be wearing the eye, but when they realised that they had lost it they cried out in alarm. Perseus then revealed his presence by speaking aloud and telling them that he had their eye, which he would return only when told how to reach the Stygian Nymphs who alone could give him the winged sandals, Hades' helmet of invisibility and a wallet in which to carry the head; for none but the Graea knew where the Stygian Nymphs lived.

This was a secret the Graea guarded closely, but they were desperate at the thought of losing their precious eye, and so told Perseus what he needed to know.

Perseus slays the Gorgon Medusa

The Stygian Nymphs lived in the land of the Hyperboreans, at the back of the North Wind, and again with Hermes to guide him, Perseus set out to see the nymphs who readily gave him the sandals, helmet and wallet he needed.

Now only one obstacle lay ahead, the greatest of them all – the slaying of the Gorgon Medusa.

The Gorgons lived together on a lonely island, surrounded only by the petrified shapes of men and beasts who had looked on them once and been turned to stone. Not a single living thing stirred beside them. Perseus donned his helmet of darkness making him invisible, and holding his shield and his sword high flew through the air with his winged sandals down to where the Gorgons slept. Then with one great and perfectly-aimed blow (his hand was guided by Athene) he cut off Medusa's head. His mission was successful! Then, somewhat to his surprise, the winged horse Pegasus and Chrysaor the warrior leapt from Medusa's body, both fully grown. These progeny had been conceived when Poseidon and Medusa had made love in Athene's temple, but for some reason had never been born.

Medusa's sisters were now disturbed from their sleep and opening their protruding eyes, saw their decapitated sister. At once they began to search for her slayer, but Perseus was well protected by his helmet of darkness and when he had tucked the head into his magic wallet, he flew quite safely away.

*

On his return journey to Seriphos Perseus saw from his vantage point in the sky a rather sorry sight. Chained to a rock jutting out of the sea below him was a beautiful young girl, crying out with terror as a sea monster circled around her drawn-up feet. At once Perseus flew down, slew the monster with his sword and gathered the girl up in his arms, very much as Heracles was later to do with Hesione (see the story of Poseidon). But unlike Heracles who was moved only by the girl's misfortune Perseus was so taken with her beauty that he fell in love. Returning with his unexpected prize to the palace he learned that the girl's name was Andromeda and that she was the daughter of the king and his boastful wife who had claimed that Andromeda was more beautiful than the Nereids. This foolish boast was repeated to Poseidon who in retaliation sent a flood and the sea monster to terrify the people, until an oracle reported that the only way to appease the sea god was to sacrifice Andromeda.

Perseus now asked the king and queen if he could marry their daughter he had saved from certain death, but although they agreed, they were not very enthusiastic for the king's brother was also in love with the girl, although he had done nothing to save her from a grisly death.

Perseus marries and returns to Seriphos

The wedding preparations went ahead, and the time for the marriage arrived. All was proceeding according to plan when suddenly the service was interrupted by the king's brother and his men who had come to claim Andromeda. Now the king too, and his wife turned on Perseus and said that he could not have Andromeda, quite forgetting it seemed that without Perseus there would have been very little of Andromeda to have.

Perseus began to fight like a hero, but lacking comrades or supporters of any sort he was hopelessly outnumbered and so was forced to hold the head of Medusa up in front of the rioting crowd, and turn them all to stone.

Then, without further delay, Perseus and Andromeda returned to Seriphos where Danaë was now hiding in the temple with Dictys (the fisherman who had found the chest so many years before.)

Polydectes had been so confident that he was sending Perseus off to certain death that he had tried at once to force Danaë to marry him. She had refused and fled to Dictys for help, then both had taken refuge in the temple, though shaking with fear as to what might follow.

Leaving his bride in Danaë's care, Perseus strode at once towards the palace where Polydectes and his favourite companions were dining. With a marvellous flourish Perseus threw open the great doors of the dining hall and then as all eyes turned towards him he addressed the horrified Polydectes saying, with no small pride, that he had brought the prize Polydectes requested. Then, without another word Perseus took Medusa's head from the wallet and held it up before the hushed crowd, who turned at once to stone, forever silenced.

The people of Seriphos were delighted with the good news, and feasting and dancing followed to celebrate not only Perseus's marriage, but also the naming by Perseus of Dictys as the new king – a unanimously popular choice.

This done Perseus, Danaë and Andromeda left Seriphos for Argos. Acrisius heard of their intended arrival and fled for Larissa. But quite by chance Perseus found himself in Larissa too, though neither king nor grandson recognised each other.

Perseus went to Larissa only because funeral games were being held and he wished to compete in the pentathlon. Perseus ran, jumped and wrestled magnificently, but when the penultimate test, the discus throwing, came round the discus he threw misfired, landed on Acrisius's foot, and killed him.

The long-ago prediction had been unwittingly fulfilled.

ITHACA

The home of Odysseus and Penelope

Note: Odysseus is frequently referred to by his latin name, Ulysses.

Despite the rumour that Pan was mothered by Penelope and fathered by the many lovers she had during Odysseus's twenty years' absence, Penelope is generally spoken of as the most faithful of wives, in fact, as a very symbol of fidelity.

In true heroic style Odysseus won Penelope in a race, run down a Spartan street. It was predicted after their marriage that if Odysseus went to Troy he would not return for twenty years so when Menelaus came to try to enlist his aid in the battle the Greeks were about to launch to win back Helen (of Troy), Odysseus attempted to pretend that he was insane, and incapable of going.

But Menelaus outwitted him for as Odysseus was ploughing his fields Menelaus threw Odysseus's son Telemachus in front of the plough. At once Odysseus ran forward to save the child, and Menelaus knew that he could not be insane.

So Odysseus went to Troy, fought valiantly, and indeed did not return to Ithaca before twenty years had passed.

During the years of Odysseus's absence Penelope was constantly courted by those who wished to marry her and to claim the throne of Ithaca. As the years went by pressure on her grew, but she was adamant that Odysseus would return and the many suitors (some say one hundred and twelve) complimented and cajoled in vain.

Finally Penelope was bound to offer some excuse other than her confident expectation of Odysseus's return, so she told her suitors that she would give them a decision when she had finished weaving the shroud for Laertes, Odysseus's father. All day Penelope would sit, diligently weaving, head bowed. But as soon as night fell she would unravel her day's work so that the shroud was never even near completion.

After three years, despite their nightly mutual entertainment and feasting, the suitors' belief in Penelope's word began to wane and they set one of her maid's to spy on her, who duly reported back that Penelope's nightwork undid that of the day.

Now that she was exposed Penelope's anxiety grew, especially as her son Telemachus had left the island in search of his father, and poor Penelope felt defenceless, and pretty desperate.

However what Penelope did not know was that Odysseus *was* home, though guided by Athene, he had been transformed into a beggar. Telemachus too had returned to Ithaca, successfully evading the suitors who, convinced now that their wait for Penelope was at an end, had planned to kill him.

Odysseus made himself known to his delighted son, though at the same time securing his promise that he would say nothing to Penelope. He then made his way to the great hall where all the suitors were gathered. Although none of his servants recognised him Odysseus was greeted with glee by his dog who had been sitting by the fire and waiting for the twenty years that Odysseus had been away. But the relief was too much for the dog, and after one eager wag of his tail, and a loving lick of Odysseus's hand, the dog lay down and died.

Odysseus spent some time in the great hall, listening to the talk of the suitors unobserved. He was most unimpressed and decided that immediate action was vital.

Word was sent to Penelope that there was an old beggar present with news of her husband, and she sent for Odysseus at once. Because he talked to her gently and kindly Penelope felt inclined to trust the man, poor and unkempt as he was, and so when Odysseus suggested to her that she should offer herself to the suitor who could string the great bow of her husband and shoot through a row of double-headed axes, Penelope decided to follow the stranger's advice.

Telemachus meanwhile removed all the suitors' weapons from the walls of the hall where they were usually hung, and locked them in the armoury, so that when the men were called to the contest, the walls were bare, though no one noticed this in the thronging and excitement.

And so the contest began, but not a single one of the suitors was able to even begin to string the bow and when finally the beggar from the corner came forward asking to take a turn the great princes who had gone before him jeered and jibed, laughing at his gall.

Their laughter ceased as Odysseus picked up the bow, strung it, and drew, sending his arrow straight through the axes. Now there was no sound at all in the hall until a gasp of horror as Odysseus sent another arrow to its mark, the neck of Antinous, chief of the suitors, who fell dead at their feet.

At once his fellow suitors stirred from their stupor and jumped to find their weapons, which, they now realised for the first time, were missing from the hall.

A great struggle followed but Odysseus, Telemachus and two faithful servants, with Athene guiding and occasionally intervening, outfought the graceless suitors who fell dead one by one, as the hall swam in their blood.

The old nurse now went running to Penelope to tell her that her husband was at home and the suitors lay in the great hall dead, but after twenty years' of waiting and hoping Penelope was disinclined to believe good news and thought that the old woman was deceiving her. But the nurse insisted, saying that she had washed Odysseus's feet and recognised an old scar, so finally Penelope allowed herself to be persuaded and followed the nurse to where Odysseus was waiting.

> Awake, Penelope, dear child, and see
> With thine own eyes what thou hast pined for long
> Ulysses has returned; thy lord is here
> Though late, and he has slain the arrogant crew
> Of suitors, who disgraced his house, and made
> His wealth a spoil, and dared insult his son.
>
> Homer (Bryant's tr.)

Odysseus was now himself again, but Penelope was bewildered, because one moment this stranger was her husband, and the next he was not. Then old Laertes was summoned and Odysseus told his father and wife of his many adventures both during the war and in the ten years that had passed since. As he spoke Penelope grew more calm, seeing in him a recognisable Odysseus again, and when he finally stopped speaking she was able to truly acknowledge and welcome him.

There was not to be a happy-ever-after ending to this reunion of lovers however, for the relatives of the dead suitors were determined to take revenge on Odysseus for his slaughter.

A judgement was passed and Odysseus was sent from Ithaca for yet another ten years; and Telemachus was appointed king in his place. Odysseus had still to appease his old adversary Poseidon and he did this by sacrificing and founding a shrine to the god.

Then, as ten years had to pass before he could return to Penelope, Odysseus married again. His bride was Callidice, Queen of the Thesprotians (now North-Western Greece, bordering Albania). After nine years with the Queen Odysseus placed their son on the throne and returned once more to Ithaca.

The island was now being ruled by Penelope in the name of a younger son, for Telemachus had left the island when an oracle had predicted that Odysseus would be killed by his son.

But it was not Telemachus who killed Odysseus but Telegonus, his son by Circe, the sorceress, who mistook Ithaca for Corfu and invaded it, unwittingly killing his father with a spear.

With Odysseus dead Telemachus came back to Ithaca, and eventually married Circe himself, while Telegonus, Circe's son, married the faithful Penelope.

CORFU

Odysseus meets Nausicaa

The story that follows is only a small part of a long adventure
saga which is the subject of an epic poem by Homer called
The Odyssey. This is certainly one of the greatest adventure
stories of all time and cannot be too highly recommended.
Recommended translations are by W. H. D. Rouse, which is
available as a Mentor paperback, and by E. V. Rieu, available
as a Penguin paperback.

When the Trojan War was over and the Greeks had taken the
city, they found Cassandra, a daughter of Priam and a prophetess,
clinging to Athena's image in the temple. But instead of respect-
ing both Cassandra and the sanctuary she had sought, the Greeks
seized her roughly and dragged her from the temple.

Athena was furious at this behaviour and went to Poseidon to
complain. His anger against the Trojans had receded now that
they had been so thoroughly defeated, and he was able to afford a
little spite against the Greeks. So when the Greeks embarked on
their voyage home, after ten long years away, Poseidon set up a
fierce storm which wrecked some boats and drove Odysseus so
far off his course that it was to be another ten years before he
again reached Ithaca, his home.

Odysseus and his men had many adventures, staying for some
time on the island of Aeaea where Odysseus had several sons
with Circe, a sorceress and perhaps a daughter of the sun. From
there they sailed past the Island of Sirens, just as Jason and the
Argonauts had done years before. Odysseus's party had no
Orpheus to distract them from the Sirens' singing so Circe had
prepared them by telling Odysseus that his men should plug their
ears with bees-wax and that if he himself wanted to hear the
music, that the men must tie him securely to the mast of the ship,

with a promise not to let him escape. They passed as planned, but the singing was so unbearably sweet that Odysseus begged and pleaded to be released to go to the Sirens, but his men refused to listen to him and only bound him tighter. When they had passed safely the Sirens were so upset at their failure to lure Odysseus that they committed suicide.

Siren.   Come, worthy Greek! Ulysses, come;
                Possess these shores with me!
           The winds and seas are troublesome
                And here we may be free.
           Here may we sit and view their toil
                That travail in the deep,
           And joy the day in mirth the while
                And spend the night in sleep.

Ulysses.   Fair nymph, if fame or honour were
                To be attained with ease,
           Then would I come and rest me there,
                And leave such toils as these.
           But here it dwells, and here must I
                With danger seek it forth:
           To spend the time luxuriously
                Becomes not men of worth.

Siren.   Ulysses, O! be not deceived
                With that unreal name;
           This honour is a thing conceived
                And rests on others' fame;
           Begotten only to molest
                Our peace, and to beguile
           The best thing of our life, our rest,
                And give us up to toil.

Ulysses.   Delicious nymph, suppose there were
                Nor honour nor report,
           Yet manliness would scorn to wear
                The time in idle sport;
           For toil doth give a better touch
                To make us feel our joy,
           And ease finds tediousness as much
                As labour yields annoy.

Samuel Daniel
(*Ulysses and the Siren*)

The next danger Odysseus had to face was sailing between Scylla, the poor creature transformed by Amphitrite, Poseidon's wife, and Charybdis, an equally hideous creature (actually a whirlpool). The child of Mother Earth and Poseidon, Charybdis sucked into herself a huge volume of water three times a day, and then spat it out again. To navigate between these two eager monsters was extraordinarily difficult and Odysseus only partly succeeded for when he had got the boat through he turned around and saw Scylla had grabbed six of his best men, holding one in each of her mouths.

Odysseus then landed in Sicily where his men grew hungry and disobeying his orders, killed some cattle belonging to Helius, the sun god. For this they were severely punished as, when they set sail again, Poseidon once more sent a storm; their ship foundered and all aboard were lost except Odysseus who drifted for nine days, grimly clinging to the mast and keel until he was washed up on the island of Ogygia.

Here he was taken in by the beautiful Calypso, a daughter of Thetis and Oceanus. She fell desperately in love with Odysseus and promised him that if he would stay with her, he would enjoy eternal youth.

Odysseus did indeed stay with Calypso for a long time, many say seven years. But he had quickly grown tired of her despite her beauty and kindness and longed to return to Ithaca.

Finally the gods took pity on him and when Poseidon was in Ethiopia, Zeus sent Hermes to tell Calypso that despite her love she must let Odysseus go.

Calypso had no choice but to obey, so sadly and slowly she told him to build a raft from twenty tree-trunks lashed together and gave him provisions for the journey. He kissed her goodbye, and set sail.

Odysseus had not been at sea for more than a day or two when Poseidon returned from Ethiopia and as he was driving his chariot across the sea he saw Odysseus sitting on his raft and at once sent a huge wave which knocked the hero off. Down to the bottom of the sea Odysseus went, heavily weighted by the luxurious robes he wore. But at last, when his lungs were close to bursting, he struggled to the surface again and clambered back onto the raft.

By now Poseidon had reached his palace in the Euboean Gulf so Athene dared to send a wind to make Odysseus's journey a little speedier. Nevertheless by the time he reached Corfu, then called the island of Drepane, he was completely exhausted and could do nothing more than to lie down beside a stream, cover himself with leaves, and go to sleep.

In the morning the daughter of the king and queen of the island came to the stream where Odysseus still slept to wash her clothes.* The girl's name was Nausicaa, which means burner of ships. She was beautiful and talented, and additionally must have had great presence of mind.

Nausicaa did not at first notice Odysseus, for despite his fatigue he had covered himself with care and looked more like a bush than a man. But later, when her work was done, Nausicaa played ball with her friends and when this bounced into the water Odysseus finally woke up.

He realised at once that he was surrounded by women and had no clothes to wear, but he improvised with an olive-branch and called softly to Nausicaa. If she was alarmed she did not show it, but listened carefully to Odysseus's story and moved by his obvious distress, took him by a discreet path to the palace.

Alcinous, Nausicaa's father, was equally kind to Odysseus and when they had listened fascinated to another telling of his marvellous story, the king plied him with gifts before arranging for a boat to carry him to Ithaca.

Odysseus was still very tired, and when the ship reached the cove of Phorcys he was still sleeping, so the sailors gently carried him off and laid him on the beach, piling Alcinous's gifts beside him.

But Poseidon managed to have the last word, for having seen the kindness these people showed to Odysseus he became very angry and changed the returning ship, and her crew, into a rock.

> He drew near
> And smote it with his open palm, and made
> The ship a rock, fast rooted in the bed
> Of the deep sea.
>
> Homer (Bryant's tr.)

Poor kindly Alcinous tried to placate the sea-god by sacrificing twelve fine bulls to him, but Poseidon returned this gesture by threatening to drop a mountain between the harbours of the city.

Note: Nausicaa is thought by Samuel Butler to be a self-portrait

* In *Prospero's Cell* Laurence Durrell claims that this spot might be one of three: Kassopi, Paleopolis or Palaiokastritsa.

of a talented Scicilian writer; a noblewoman who lived in the Eryx district. He made her the subject of a study entitled *Authoress of the Odyssey* and concluded (as had Apollodorus) that the *Odyssey* was an account of a voyage around Sicily.

A quite different book which suggests that the Odyssey was a journey beyond the Mediterranean, to Scotland and perhaps even to Iceland, is Gilbert Pillot's *Secret Code of the Odyssey* (Abelard-Schuman). This is a fascinating proposition and Pillot argues his case in a way that is both plausible and entertaining.

JASON AND THE ARGONAUTS

Phrixus is snatched

The story of the search by Jason and the Argonauts for the Golden Fleece must begin with King Athamas who grew tired of his first wife Nephele, and divorced her so that he could marry Ino, a daughter of Cadmus of Thebes.

Nephele had two children by the King and her son Phrixus was rightful heir, but Nephele rightly assumed that Ino would certainly bear children of her own and would want them to inherit, and so the child's life was in danger.

Ino came from a scrupulously fair family, but her greed for power overcame her and she planned a subtle and devious way to get rid of Phrixus. Before the men went to sow their corn, she dried it out and so of course no crops appeared. When the men in their distress turned to the king for advice he consulted an oracle and Ino bribed the messenger to tell the king that the only sacrifice which would satisfy the gods would be the killing of Phrixus. The king heard the news with horror, for he loved the child and like all Greeks regarded human sacrifice as abhorrent, but the people were starving and desperate, and forced him to follow what they took to be the gods' instructions.

The boy was taken to the altar and laid down on it, but before a knife could be put to his throat a ram with a shining fleece of pure gold snatched the boy up, and also his sister, Helle, and took them away to Colchis.

On the journey however, as they crossed the narrow strait between Europe and Asia Minor (now called Dardanelles Strait), Helle fell into the water and was drowned. The strait was then named Hellespont in her honour, which means the sea of Helle.

Where beauteous Helle found a watery grave.
Meleager

When he had safely arrived in Colchis (on the shores of the Black Sea) Phrixus sacrificed the ram to Zeus, and presented the King, Aeëtes, a son of the sun-god Helius, with the invaluable Golden Fleece.

*   *   *

Phrixus had an uncle named Aeson who was the rightful heir to the Iolcan throne in Thessaly, but Aeson had been usurped from his rightful inheritance by his half-brother, Pelias. An oracle warned Pelias that he would be killed by a descendant of Aeolus – Aeson's forebear – so Pelias promptly had all Aeolians killed, although out of respect for their mother, he spared Aeson himself.

Aeson's wife, Polymele, was now pregnant and Pelias was determined to kill the child as soon as it was born, but Polymele outwitted him for when she gave birth to her strong healthy son she and her women leant over the baby, weeping and lamenting that he had been still-born. So Pelias was no longer interested and under the pretext of burying the child, Polymele had him smuggled out to the care of Cheiron, King of the Centaurs. Half horse and half man, Cheiron was as renowned for his kindness and wisdom as his fellow Centaurs were for their riotous and disreputable behaviour.

And so Jason grew up in Thessaly, safe from harm.

Meanwhile Pelias had a second message from the oracle, telling him to beware a man wearing only one sandal, for this man would be the cause of his death. Of course he referred to Jason, who in due course did appear in Iolcus with only one sandal. He had lost the other when, as he stood on the banks of the River Anaurus, he had noticed an old woman who was begging to be carried across the water, but whose pleas were ignored or refused by those around her. So Jason called out to her that he would help, but was astonished when he lifted her onto his back to find out how heavy she was for in fact the old woman was none other than Hera herself in disguise. Under her weight he stumbled a little, losing a sandal in the rushing water.

When Jason reached the home of Pelias, whom he did not yet recognise, news had already reached the king of a marvellously beautiful man, with long bright hair which hung freely down his back. The country people were even saying that it might be Apollo himself. Pelias was extremely curious about this person, but when Jason appeared in front of him wearing just one sandal Pelias's curiosity turned to fear and he asked Jason what he would do if

faced with the prophecy that one of his citizens was to kill him.
Jason's reply, inspired by Hera, was that he would send this
person to Colchis in search of the Golden Fleece. Jason then
went on to ask Pelias for his name, and when he heard it boldly
declared that it was to see Pelias that he had come, for he wished
to claim the throne himself.

Pelias was inwardly in a turmoil, but displayed a cool calm as
he agreed that Jason had a fair claim, but that before he could
rule the people, he must free them of the curse of the ghost of
Phrixus by bringing back to Iolcus the Golden Fleece and freeing
the spirit of Phrixus who had not been buried by the Colchians
with the proper rites.

Both Pelias and Jason knew that the Fleece was guarded by a
thousand-coiled dragon which never slept and that Jason was
being asked to perform a near impossible task, but he nevertheless
responded to it with a hero's love of adventure, and accepted with
enthusiasm and grace.

Jason sent messengers to every corner of Greece, summoning
the great heroes to come to help him with his task, and his ship
Argo was built by the great shipbuilder Argus under the direction
of Athene who herself placed in the prow an oracular beam.

The brave young men of Greece began to arrive, about fifty in
all, sharing with Jason the thrill of this adventure against such
heavy odds. Among those who came were Castor and Polydeuces, Meleager of Calydon, Orpheus, Peleus, Atalanta, the only
girl in the party, and Heracles who interrupted his Labours to
come to take part.* All agreed that Heracles should lead the
party, for his own amazing exploits were well known, but
Heracles refused, saying that this was Jason's expedition and that
Jason himself must lead it.

First Stop, the Island of Lemnos

When the boat was finally ready and the men and Atalanta had
taken their places aboard, they set a course for the island of
Lemnos.

This was an island peopled only by women, for the previous
year their men had come back with Thracian women captured as
booty and publicly declared that they preferred these strangers to
their own wives (who were reputed to smell). The women were

* Stories of all these figures are recounted in *Land of Zeus*.

enraged by this insult and collectively planned to kill the men. This they did, all except their leader Hypsipyle who could not bear to kill her father, the king, and instead set him adrift in an oarless boat, with only the chance of death ahead. (He was in fact, cast ashore on the island of Sicinos.) She did this in secret however, and as far as the Lemnian women knew, every one of the Lemnian men was dead.

When the women saw the *Argo* approaching their island they put on their armour and prepared to fight again, thinking it was an enemy ship from Thrace. But Jason sent them a charming messenger and the women gave up the idea of fighting, and sent food to the ship.

It was while the *Argo* was still in the harbour, and the men on board, that Hypsipyle's wise old nurse pointed out that the Lemnians were in danger of becoming extinct as they now had no men to further their race. A boat full of men was in the harbour, perhaps, she suggested, the women should invite them to the city for some days of love making to ensure the continuation of their race.

The women thought this an excellent suggestion and immediately acted on it, taking the men to their homes and treating them with every kindness. Jason himself stayed with Hypsipyle and she conceived twin sons, one of whom would later become king of Lemnos and was to supply the Greeks with wine during the Trojan War.

The Argonauts might well have stayed on Lemnos forever, but Heracles had stayed behind to watch the *Argo* and did not take part in the general merry making. Soon he came banging on doors and calling to the Argonauts, reminding them of the task that lay ahead, and so they reassembled at the harbour.

From Samothrace to the Sea of Marmara

When the Argonauts reached Samothrace Orpheus suggested they should be initiated into the strange, mysterious rites of the island, which would protect them from shipwreck. This done they sailed on towards the Hellespont.

This important strait was well guarded by King Laomedon of Troy, and no Greek ships were permitted to pass through it. But refusing to be daunted, the Argonauts made the treacherous passage by night, moving carefully along the coast of Thrace and reaching the Sea of Marmara without incident.

They next took shelter in the harbour of Cyzicus where the king greeted them with delight and asked them to join his wedding festivities which were in progress. The Argonauts enthusiastically accepted the generous invitation, but while they were celebrating with the king and his bride, the *Argo* was attacked by six-armed giants, enemies of the king.

The guards were successful in beating off the giants, but as soon as the Argonauts returned to their ship they decided to set sail, marking out a course to take them to the Bosphorous. During the night however a storm blew up, and the Argonauts were forced to turn their ship back, landing at an unknown beach.

There they were immediately attacked by skilled fighting men, though neither side could see their assailants in the darkness. The Argonauts fought bravely, and their attackers soon fell dead, or ran for safety. But when dawn broke the Argonauts saw that they had been killing their hosts of the previous day, and that at their feet lay the king, dead.

The sad news was carried to Cleite, his wife of one day, and in her sorrow she hanged herself. The nymphs of the woods were so moved by her grief that they wept copiously, their tears turning into a fountain which bears Cleite's name.

To Colchis via the Black Sea

The Argonauts were becalmed in the Sea of Marmara for many days, and during this time took part in funeral games in honour of King Cyzicus.

At the suggestion of Heracles, the Argonauts now took part in a rowing contest which, though it was started in high humour and and good spirits, quickly became something rather more serious, even ominous. Finally only the twins Castor and Polydeuces, also known as the Dioscuri. Jason, and Heracles were able to continue to row, and then when Castor grew tired and Polydeuces stopped rowing to save his brother's waning strength, the contest was reduced to one between Jason and Heracles only. Orpheus tried to relieve the tension with his music, but the two heroes were not to be distracted. Finally Jason could bear the strain no longer, and from sheer exhaustion he fainted. Heracles was now the winner, but before he had rowed another stroke, his oar snapped in two.

The *Argo* was now pulled into land, and Heracles went in search of a tree which he could pull out of the ground to make a new oar. While Heracles was doing this his young friend, a lovely boy named Hylas, was searching for water. When some hours had passed and Hylas did not return Heracles became worried and the Argonauts spread out in several directions to search for Hylas, calling his name, but without success.

Heracles was almost beside himself with worry when one of the Argonauts came to him with the news that he had heard Hylas calling for help, but that when he followed the direction of his voice the boy was not there, though his empty water pitcher lay on the ground. The only conclusion they could reach was that the nymphs too had been charmed by the boy's beauty and had dragged him into the water with them.

This story in no way appeased Heracles' fears for Hylas, and he refused to give up his own search. The Argonauts had all by now drifted back to the *Argo* and when Heracles did not return, they sailed on without him. But Heracles searched on in vain.

Some said that Jason made the decision to leave Heracles behind because he was piqued that he had lost the rowing contest. Certainly Heracles was angry at their betrayal and later killed two of the Argonauts who had supported the decision to leave him.

Without Heracles the Argonauts went on once more, landing briefly at the island of Bebrycos, still in the Sea of Marmara where Polydeuces defeated an evil king in a boxing contest and then landing at a coastal port where they were met by a most unfortunate man named Phineus. This man had been given the gift of prophecy but had used it so effectively that he had angered the gods, and particularly Zeus, and so Phineus had lost his sight, and worse, was constantly plagued by creatures called Harpies. These were females of sorts, who were winged and could fly through the air. Wherever they went they left behind them a foul smell and every time that poor Phineus sat down to eat his meal the Harpies would swoop down and grab his food, eating most of it and fouling the scraps they left behind, making them stinking, rotten and inedible. Phineus was now more than half starved, and quite desperate. So when the Argonauts asked for his help to get them to the Golden Fleece, Phineus was forced to make a bargain with them. If they could rid him of the Harpies, he would give them invaluable guidance to overcome the dangers that lay between them and their goal.

Aboard the *Argo* were two sons of Boreas, the North Wind. They too were winged and Phineus knew that they alone could save him from the loathsome curse.

Food was put out, and at once the Harpies came down out of the sky, gobbling and cackling and leaving their smell which was so strong it made men sick. Then, as they flew back into the sky, Boreas's sons followed them with their swords. On and on the Harpies flew with their pursuers close behind, ready to kill them. But before this could be done, Hera's messenger, Iris, came to save them, saying that their lives should be spared, and she would see to it that they did not return to plague Phineus again.

Phineus's gratitude was profound, and he was delighted to give the Argonauts detailed instructions to help them through the Bosphorous, and on to Colchis. At their destination, he said, they would be guided by Aphrodite.

The way through the Bosphorous was almost impassable for the entrance alone was always shrouded in a heavy mist, and on either side of the entrance stood Clashing Rocks which rocked perpetually together so that when a ship tried to pass between, it would be horribly crushed.

So, to fly in ahead of them, the Argonauts released a dove because Phineus had told them that if the dove flew through and returned to them, they too would pass through the rocks in safety. If the dove did not return, then he would have to give up all hope of reaching Colchis and the Golden Fleece.

There was silence on the *Argo* as the Argonauts waited for the dove to return. The rocks ahead seemed so treacherous and the waves so high that they could scarcely imagine that it was possible for the little dove to escape death. But equally they found it impossible to believe that having come so far, rowed so hard, overcome such dangers, that their quest could now fail. And so they sat, their oars idle and their eyes searching the sky for the returning dove.

At last they were rewarded! Back flew the white dove, quite safe and unharmed except for her tail feathers which had been clipped as the rocks had rolled together.

Now the rowers took up their oars again and with all their mighty combined strength took the *Argo* swiftly through the treacherous entrance, timing their passage so exactly that they shot through in the brief moments when the rocks were parted. Only the tail end of the stern was caught and damaged, just as the tail feathers had been caught and snipped from the dove.

Since this time the rocks have been steady, and boats have been free to pass through the Bosphorous without danger.

*

Now the Argonauts went on through the Black Sea, along the coast of Asia Minor, until they reached the small island of Thynias where they had a vision of Apollo and made their great vow never to desert each other in time of danger.

From Thynias they went to Mariandyne which is famous because it was near here that Heracles found the chasm through which he dragged the three headed dog Cerberus from the Underworld up to Eurystheus when he was performing his labours.

Sinope was their next stop. This city was named in honour of a girl who outwitted both Zeus and Apollo who were in love with her and longed to possess her but when Zeus promised that he would give her anything she wanted she replied that all she longed for was perpetual virginity, and of course he had to grant her this or break his promise, but was, therefore, never able to make love to her.

A little further along the coast was the home of the Amazons, fearless women who lived without men. Here the Argonauts did not stop, but sailed on past until they reached the island of Ares where they were attacked by Ares' birds who rained down on their heads sharp, dangerous, bronze feathers. But the Argonauts outwitted the birds by holding shields over their heads, so that the feathers bounced off. When the birds had been driven away, the *Argo* was brought into shore, and there they met up with the four sons of Phrixus and Chalciope, daughter of Aeetes, who had been on their way to Greece, but had been shipwrecked. When they heard that the Argonauts planned to go to Colchis in search of the Fleece they were at first horrified, for they knew their grandfather, Aeetes, would do all he could to keep the Golden Fleece, whatever the cost.

Their quandary was great for while they longed to honour their dead father Phrixus, and join the Argonauts in their rightful quest, they feared their grandfather and his retribution for their disloyalty to him.

But honour won, and the four joined Jason and his crew sailing with them on past the island of Philyra, birthplace of Cheiron, leader of the Centaurs; and then finally to Colchis.

Seizing the Golden Fleece

Before marching to the city gates, the Argonauts spent a night hidden in a quiet backwater where together they discussed their plans for the great task that lay ahead.

Consultations were taking place in Olympus too, for the gods fully realised that the brave band of Argonauts had still to overcome enormous odds before their quest would be completed. Hera and Athene were especially anxious that the Argonauts should succeed. So much so, that Hera overcame her usual haughty attitude towards Aphrodite and went to the goddess of love to ask her to help by sending her son Eros to shoot an arrow through the heart of Medea, King Aeetes' daughter, for if she fell in love with Jason, the Argonaut's would have an invaluable ally.

Medea, a witch-priestess of Hecate, goddess of witches, was one of two daughters born to King Aeetes by his first wife. The other, Chalciope, was Phrixus's widow. King Aeetes had now married again, and by his second wife, Eidyia, he had a son named Apsyrtus.

As the Argonauts made their approach to the city they were met first by Chalciope. Her four sons told her of their rescue from the island of Ares by the Argonauts, and then as Aeetes and Eidyia joined them the story was told again, although this time the young men added that the Argonauts had come in search of the Fleece as an oracle had predicted.

Aeetes was furious at their very presence, for he had tried to keep all Greeks away from the Black Sea, and when he heard their reason for coming he very nearly exploded with rage, and ordered the Argonauts to return, warning them that if they did not he would cut off their hands and cut out their tongues.

At this point Medea joined the group and Aeetes, who was ashamed to display his rudeness in front of his daughter, changed his mind and said that the Argonauts could have the Fleece, on condition that Jason could yoke together two bulls with breath of fire, and bronze feet, and use them to plough a field. When the field was ploughed Jason was to plant serpent's teeth, from which would grow armed men, just as Cadmus did when founding Thebes.

Jason was astounded and dismayed at Aeetes' suggestion for he did not know that Eros had already sent an arrow into Medea's heart, and that she was making her plans to help him.

Together Medea and Chalciope discussed what had to be done, and finally Medea sent her sister to Jason to tell him of her love and to say that she would help him on condition that Jason took her with the Argonauts when the *Argo* left, and that she would become Jason's bride.

Jason readily agreed to Medea's request, and seriously and

solemnly promised that he would always be faithful to her. She then gave him a charm, a lotion made from the blood-red juice of the flower which had sprung up from the blood of Prometheus when it dripped down onto earth. (Some say Prometheus created man out of clay and first gave him fire – which angered Zeus who punished him foully.) If Jason would rub this lotion all over his body, it would protect him from the burning heat of the bulls' breath.

Two Argonauts were sent to the *Argo* to collect the dragon's teeth, then as his companions stood by wishing him well, Jason began his task.

The bulls were loosened and rushed towards him, breathing fire that would have killed a man in seconds, but Medea's potion served Jason well and he stood his ground till he had the beasts bridled, and then ploughed the field as Aeetes had instructed him, though never expecting that Jason would actually succeed.

When the ploughing was completed, Jason buried the dragon's teeth deeply into the furrows and almost at once armed men rose up, bristling with aggression and ready to turn at once to attacking Jason.

The hero had however been warned of this eventuality too by the redoubtable Medea, and picking up a large stone he had moved during his ploughing, he threw it between the men who immediately lost interest in Jason and began to fight each other. Finally only a few were left, and these Jason sent off to attend their wounds, while he returned in triumph to King Aeetes, ready to claim the Golden Fleece.

King Aeetes was not, however, in the least willing to share Jason's elation; nor was he prepared to keep his word. Shamelessly and boldly he refused to honour his promise and instead vowed to himself that he would burn the *Argo* and kill all the Argonauts. He did not yet suspect Medea's connivence in Jason's victory, and now again confided in her, telling his daughter of his ugly plans to finish off the Argonauts and their quest.

Medea listened without comment, merely nodding from time to time as she took careful note of what her father told her. Then, when she could reasonably be excused, she ran as fast as was possible to where the *Argo* was moored, and told Jason every word of Aeetes' plans.

At once the Argonauts were on the alert, and when Medea suggested that she should lead them without delay to the precinct of Ares where the Fleece was hung, they agreed with alacrity.

So the *Argo* slipped quietly out of Aea where it had been

moored and sailed the six miles towards their goal – the Golden Fleece.

The tree on which the Fleece hung was guarded by a hideous dragon, larger even than the *Argo* itself. It hissed and spat and was monstrously frightening, but Medea came to the Argonauts' aid by singing a sweet magical song which soothed the dragon, and finally sent it to sleep.

The very second that the dragon's eyes were closed, Jason rushed to the tree and lifted the Golden Fleece from it, holding it high as he ran to the rejoicing Argonauts.

> Exulting Jason grasped the shining hide,
> His last of labours, and his envied pride.
> Slow from the groaning branch the fleece was rent
>
> Flaccus (Elton's tr.)

But their troubles were not yet over, for the King had now learned of their absence and had sent his great army in pursuit. It seemed once more that the Argonauts must be defeated for their one small boat and tiny crew was no match for Aeetes' men. It was, however, once more a tactic of Medea which saved the party.

On board with her she had brought her young half-brother, Apsyrtus, and as her father's ships followed the *Argo* in hot pursuit, she killed her brother quickly, then cut his body into small pieces which she dropped one by one into the sea. The king and his men were forced to pick up each piece so that they could give the boy a decent burial, and as they searched for this portion or that, the Argonauts got further and further ahead, until Aeetes could no longer reach them.

Returning via Corcyra (Corfu) and Crete

The *Argo* returned through the Black Sea, the Bosphorous and the Sea of Marmara, the way it had come. The Argonauts were able to pass through the Hellespont without fear of attack as during their time at Colchis Heracles had been offended by king Laomedon, and had sacked and razed the city of Troy.

Jason and Medea left their companions for some time to go to visit Circe, Medea's aunt, who was to purify them for their crime of killing Apsyrtus; but they were collected again at Aeaea.

By the time the Argonauts reached Corcyra, their Colchian pursuers had again caught them up and begged the King and Queen of Corcyra to give them both the Fleece and Medea to take back to Aeetes. The queen was however sympathetic towards the young couple, and pleaded for them with her husband. Finally he agreed that Medea would be returned only if she was still a virgin, so that very night Jason and Medea married, and after celebrating the event with the Argonauts, spent their wedding night lying on the Golden Fleece.

Some Colchians were so delighted by the beauty of Corcyra that they chose to settle there, rather than to return to their own land.

The next hazard the Argonauts had to contend with was the lures from the Island of Sirens, where bird-women sang so beautifully that men were drawn towards them, only to find that their ship smashed on the treacherous rocks. But even their exquisite music was no match for Orpheus, and he played his lyre so magnificently that the Siren's song failed to move the heroes, with the exception of Butes who leapt over the side of the boat but who was himself rescued from the rocks as he swam towards the island by Aphrodite, who took him off to be her lover.

> And the Sirens, taught to kill
>   With their sweet voice,
> Make every echoing rock reply.
>
>   Thomas Campion

When the Argonauts wanted to stop at Crete they were prevented from doing so by a bronze giant named Talos. He had been made by Hephaestus and had been given by Zeus either to Minos or Europa to guard the island. This he did most effectively by hurling rocks at anyone who tried to approach. He walked around Crete three times a day, and if he did come across a trespasser, he would burn the stranger to death.

But even Talos had a vulnerable spot, for in his ankle was a pin and if that pin were to be pulled out, the liquid which passed for blood in his body would all escape, and he would die. This was not considered very important however, for no one dared approach him, much less go close enough to pull a tiny pin from his huge ankle.

Again it was to Medea that the Argonauts turned, and once more she did not fail them. Standing high in the prow of the ship she called to Talos that she could make him immortal if only he would drink a potion she had prepared for him. Talos was delighted to accept, and drank the potion in one gulp, but far from making him immortal, it merely sent him to sleep. Medea then went to the shore and pulled the pin from the giant, who died as the life-giving liquid trickled from his great body.

From Crete the heroes went to Aegina, and from there they made the easy journey to Iolcus and the beach of Pagasae.

Meanwhile back in Thessaly much had been happening, for the Argonauts had long since been presumed and pronounced dead. Pelias had been so emboldened by the thought of Jason's death that he had killed Jason's father and mother, Aeson and Poly-mele, and also their infant son Promachus, whose brains he beat out on the ground.

Revolted and distressed by this news, the Argonauts wanted to take immediate revenge on Pelias, but Medea again intervened and said she could best handle matters alone.

Disguised as an old crone, and accompanied by her women dressed as she was in strange garb, Medea approached the city and seeking out Pelias's daughters she told them that it was within her power to rejuvenate their father who was now fast approaching old age.

The girls at once took her to Pelias who viewed Medea's claims with some scepticism, but when first Medea turned herself young before his eyes, and then a ram was transformed (Medea in fact had a newly-born lamb kept hidden in the folds of her cloak) his misgivings vanished, and he placed himself in Medea's hands, believing that as she claimed, he was to be honoured by Artemis through Medea's ministrations.

Medea told the king to lie on his couch, and lulled him quickly to sleep with one of her very special songs. She then ordered his daughters to cut him into small pieces, just as they had seen her do to the ram which they had presumed she was really transforming. In all good faith they fell to their task, and threw the small pieces into a boiling cauldron which they then carried onto the top of the roof. The light from the torches lit on the roof was the signal that the Argonauts had been expecting, and they at once rushed into the city where they met a population too shaken to resist their plans to take over.

Pelias's son Acastus, was not prepared to let Jason take the throne, and as Jason felt confident that even greater wealth and honour were available for him elsewhere, he and

Medea went into exile, going first to Boeotia, where he left the Golden Fleece in a temple dedicated to Zeus, then finally to Corinth where Jason became king.

Note: In *The Greek Myths* Vol. 2, Robert Graves notes Sir Isaac Newton's observation of the connection between the Zodiac and the *Argo*'s voyage, and says: 'the legend may well have been influenced at Alexandria by the Zodiacal Signs: the Ram of Phrixus, the Bulls of Aeetes, the Dioscuri as the Heavenly Twins, Rhea's lion, the Scales of Alcinous, the Water-carriers of Aegina, Heracles as Bowman, Medea as Virgin, and the Goat, symbol of lechery, to record the love-making on Lemnos. When the Egyptian Zodiacal Signs are used, the missing elements appear: Serpent (dragon) for Scorpion; and Scarab, symbol of regeneration, for Crab.'

JASON AND MEDEA

For ten years Jason and Medea lived happily together in Corinth, and together they had fourteen children. Then Jason began to accuse his wife of having poisoned Corinthus, heir to the throne before Jason began his rule (who had indeed died opportunely), to secure the prize of the throne for Jason himself. Along with these accusations Jason sneakily introduced his plan to divorce Medea in order that he might marry Glauce, the daughter of King Creon the Theban.

Medea reminded her husband again and again of all he owed her, and of his promise made in Colchis that he would always be faithful to her; but Jason was captivated by Glauce and determined. He knew perfectly well that Medea's probable poisoning of Corinthus had been entirely on his behalf, but piously chose to forget this fact.

Medea argued and pleaded, but when she saw that Jason was unmoved she pretended to accede with his demands and as soon as he was married sent her seven sons to present Glauce with gifts, a beautiful white robe and a richly ornamented golden crown.

The bride was delighted with Medea's kindness and tolerance in a difficult situation and put on the dress and placed the crown on her head. But no sooner had she done so than she was consumed by flames which killed not only Glauce but all those gathered within the burning palace, including King Creon. Only Jason was able to jump out of the window to safety.

The years that lay ahead were not particularly happy for either Medea or Jason. Medea later married the king of Athens, but was banished for attempting to poison Theseus;* then she fled to Asia where she married again and finally back to Colchis where she helped Aeetes to regain his throne. However her end was a happy one for she was granted immortality, and so never

ed but was instead taken to the Elysian Fields where some say
e became Achilles' bride.

Jason wandered, miserable and wretched, from place to place
ntil he was an old man. He then returned to Corinth to sit beside
e *Argo*, reliving his past glories. His grief at the contrast be-
ween his splendid early years and his recent years of misery was
great that he planned to hang himself, but before he could do
, the prow fell from the ship and killed him, painlessly and
stantly.

This story is told in greater detail in the section entitled: The Naming of
e Aegean.

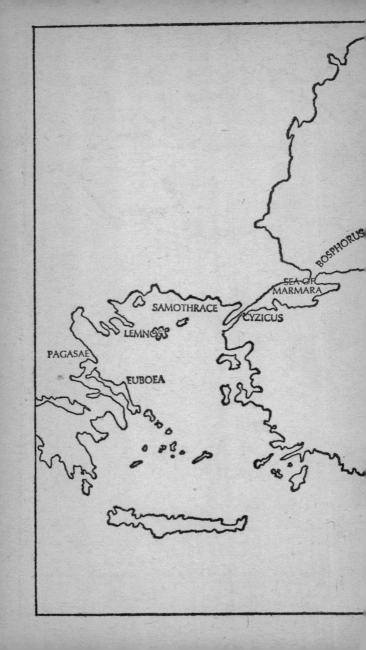

CK SEA

COLCHIS

SINOPE

ISLE OF ARES

TRAPEZUS

JOURNEY OF
THE ARGONAUTS

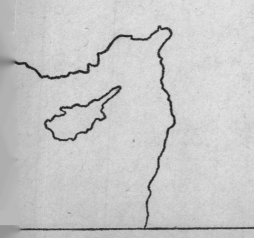